Everyday Comforts

365 Days of Life-Saving Enlightenments

By Lisa Choh

ISBN: 978-1-4525-6223-0 (sc)
ISBN: 978-1-4525-6224-7 (e)

Balboa Press books may be ordered through booksellers or by contacting:

Balboa Press
A Division of Hay House
1663 Liberty Drive
Bloomington, IN 47403
www.balboapress.com
1-(877) 407-4847

Printed in the United States of America

Balboa Press rev. date: 11/20/2012

Acknowledgements

I would like to thank my son Jason for planting and promoting the idea for this book four years ago. Your constant encouragement has now become a reality!

Thank you my dear loving son.

Also I would like to acknowledge and thank Caroline Lee and Jennifer Park for assisting me with their insightful editorial skills.

Thank you both very much.

*All bible verses are taken from the NIV (New International Version) Bible, the Amplified Bible, and the One Year Bible.

Forward

2 Corinthians 2:3-5 [3] **Praise be to the God and Father of our Lord Jesus Christ, the Father of compassion and the God of all comfort,** [4] **who comforts us in all our troubles, so that we can comfort those in any trouble with the comfort we ourselves receive from God.** [5] **For just as we share abundantly in the sufferings of Christ, so also our comfort abounds through Christ.**

A few years ago, Lisa fell off her bike and suffered a bad concussion. It was one of the darkest times of our lives. She was sleeping up to 16 hours a day but the doctor didn't want her to rest too much, and encouraged her to exercise her brain. So, Lisa started writing articles about God. She had no training in theology and had no writing experience, but this was a way for her to exercise her mind.

From the articles, she began writing daily emails to friends and family about God and His Son Jesus. During the dark months of her life, Lisa wrote of God's comfort every single day through His Spirit. It's been a blessing to us (her family and community) to see her spread God's comfort in many people's lives.

May this book help those of you who might need a little comfort; a comfort that abounds through Christ.

Pastor Andy Choh

Introduction

Our God is so good and He wants us to enjoy our lives to the fullest. This book of encouragements will help us to focus on God and His word to help us with the life issues we come across and face on a daily basis.

I pray that each page of this book can encourage you to enhance three key ingredients in your life: faith, hope and love. We can depend on these fruits of the spirit to deal with the many challenges we go through in our lives.

I also pray that the Holy Spirit will enlighten you as you read, ponder and apply His truth in wisdom. God Bless You!

Gratefully,

Lisa

Day 1
GOD, OUR SOURCE OF ALL COMFORT

Who do you go to when you're feeling down? In times of distress, can you imagine being comforted by someone who knows you well personally, inside and out, who loves you and has deep sympathy for what you're going through, who genuinely cares about you and your well-being and encourages you in all manner? You don't have to explain a thing because God is our source of comfort.

2 Corinthians 1:3-4 Blessed be the God and Father of our Lord Jesus Christ, the Father of sympathy and the God (Who is the Source) of every comfort (consolation and encouragement), Who comforts (consoles and encourages) us in every trouble (calamity and affliction), so that we may also be able to comfort those who are in any kind of trouble or distress, with the comfort with which we ourselves are comforted by God.

God gives us examples on how to comfort and encourage others. Though we sympathize with those who are suffering, we are better able at helping people when we empathize with them, for we ourselves have experienced similar situations. Let us use all that we have learned from God's divine comfort through His Holy Spirit to help others in need. However, no matter how well people become at consoling each other, remember that God is the best consoler. Where people fall short, He will never disappoint us in any way. Pray and go to God as your ultimate source of comfort. He will use different means possible to help you in times of distress. The Spirit reminds us of all of God's truth and fills you with His warm embrace.

Have the most comforting day!

Day 2
HOW LONG SHOULD WE ENDURE DISTRESS AND SUFFERINGS?

Have you ever felt deep anguish and distress in troubled times? When we feel any kind of pain, we tend to wallow in self pity or seek instant relief. But God has made and fashioned us to be stronger than that; it's a wonder how much we can handle. You will be surprised! Only God knows how much we can tolerate as individuals.

Psalm 6:3-4 My (inner) self (as well as my body) is also exceedingly disturbed and troubled. But you, O Lord, how long (until you return and speak peace to me)? Return (to my relief), O Lord, deliver my life; save me for the sake of Your steadfast love and mercy.

God has a good plan for you, and we have to trust in His sovereignty. As you call on Him, be still and know that God is listening to you. Wait and trust in His timing to help deliver you from distress. Remember, God is our potter and He has a masterpiece of art working in you. When we get uncomfortable and things don't go our way, trust that God has a perfect plan with purpose for your life. He is always there to comfort, guide, and give you His peace at all times.

When you hang in there, your faith will skyrocket and your character will strengthen as it becomes more stable. Trust God and wait on His perfect timing! It is worth it, as He loves you so and has nothing but good planned for you.

Have an enlightening day!

Day 3
FOUR PRICELESS NAMES OF GOD

What type of names could people give to you that would describe and represent who you are? In the book of Isaiah, God has four priceless names.

Isaiah 9:6 For unto us a Child is born, to us a Son is given; and the government shall be upon His shoulder, and His name shall be called wonderful counselor, mighty God, everlasting father, prince of peace.

Let's examine the names.

> **Wonderful counselor**: Wonderful in counsel, who gives the right advice with magnificent wisdom.
> **Mighty God**: The highest authority in the universe; strong, able, and powerful.
> **Everlasting Father:** Infinite. He will always be with us and we can depend on Him for His eternal Fatherly care and protection.
> **Prince of Peace**: One who brings a perfect, tranquil, steady peace to the world.

Think about the deep meaning of all four of His names. All we can say is "Wow" and have tears of joy. There is absolutely no reason to fear whatsoever! If we truly believe in these names of our God, there is nothing but hope, reassurance, guidance, and everyday strength given to us by Him. Let us remember to look back at God's past faithfulness, deliverance, and providence, so that we can continue to walk with Him daily and move forward in faith!

Have a promising day!

Day 4
SOMETHING NEW EVERY MORNING

How would you like to get something new every morning? I sure would, sounds great to me!

Lamentations 3:21-23 But this I recall and therefore have I hope and expectation: It is because of the Lord's mercy and loving-kindness that we are not consumed, because His (tender) compassions fail not. They are new every morning; great and abundant is Your stability and faithfulness.

My goodness! What would become of us if it wasn't for God's great mercy and loving-kindness every day? He knows that we make daily mistakes and are not perfect. Therefore, He offers us His tender compassion steadily by His faithfulness to us. When we think of all his goodness, knowing that we don't deserve it, we are filled with hope and expectation every morning! As God shows us His mercy and kindness, let us also let it flow through us to others.

2 Corinthians 4:16 Therefore we do not lose heart. Though outwardly we are wasting away, yet inwardly we are being renewed day by day.

Let us be thankful for God's wonderful gifts every morning! Praise God for our renewal every day, in every way.

Have a thankful day!

Day 5
GET READY FOR A BIG HAUL OF BLESSINGS

Is anyone interested in being bewildered with amazement? How about desiring to see God work beyond what you could have imagined? Well, get ready!

Luke 5:4-5 When he had finished speaking, he said to Simon, "Put out into deep water, and let down the nets for a catch." Simon answered, "Master, we've worked hard all night and haven't caught anything. But because you say so, I will let down the nets.

God wants us to take action! How difficult it can be when things don't make any sense in our lives and we're just too tired to simply obey God's word.

Luke 5:9 For he and all his companions were astonished at the catch of fish they had taken.

Imagine how Peter must have felt when he saw the great haul of fish. He must have been glad that he didn't pass on the opportunity to see a spectacular miracle right before his eyes! A wonderful part of your own relationship with God is to experience God's greatness and goodness in your life. When our flesh is weak, disheartened, or ready to give up, remember God's words of truth and obey.

Let us be encouraged to step out of ourselves, take the bold steps of faith and move forward in the right direction as God leads us with the Spirit. As we courageously do our part, get ready for a big haul of blessings.

Have a courageous day!

Day 6
LET GO FOR THE NEW

Think about the meaning of the word *new*. Excitement comes within and great expectations come forth! When children receive a new toy, they are filled with happiness and joy and cannot wait to use it! When we meet new people, get a new position or receive new possessions, we anticipate that they meet all our wonderful expectations! It's a new year!

Isaiah 43:18-19   Do not (earnestly) remember the former things; neither consider the things of old. Behold, I am doing a new thing!

We are all in wonder of new things and having a New Year ahead of us, let's be encouraged to let go of the past so we can move forward in our lives! If we hold on too tightly to the things of old and are set in our ways of comfort, it will be difficult to be in the position of receiving new ventures laid out before us from God. Trust in him and be bold, courageous, and step out to experience all of God's goodness He has planned out for you.

I pray that with faith we would release past hurts, disappointments, failings, resentments, and hardships and bury them. Then we can step forward, embrace new beginnings and have a fresh start with the abundant, blessed life that God promises for each and every one of us! God thrives on giving us new things, but He's waiting for us to do our part and let go of the past.

Have a decisive day!

Day 7
STIR UP YOUR FIRE

Do you realize what kind of power you have within you? Everything about God is good and His Spirit lives inside you. God wants us to activate His love so that we can have a balanced mind, discipline and self-control. He does not want it to lay dormant within you; He wants us to practice and use it daily!

2 Timothy 1:6-7 For this reason I remind you to fan into flame the gift of God, which is in you through the laying on of my hands. For God did not give us a spirit of timidity, but a spirit of power, of love and of self-discipline.

When you find yourself in fear, cowardly or timid, know that it definitely is not from God! Our enemy wants to use it to control us and eventually take over the great power of God from within. Stand up against that and don't let him win! We are more than conquerors through Christ who gives us strength every day!

Colossians 2:10 And you have been given fullness in Christ, who is the head over every power and authority.

So therefore, use His strength to stir up and keep burning with the gracious gifts of God, the inner fire that is in you. Remember who and whose you are: a child of the Living God most High!

Have a productive day!

Day 8
BUT I WANT IT THIS WAY

It is very important to trust in God's ways and sovereignty. When we are being lead by His Spirit to go into a certain direction, many times it may not make any sense to us at all. God does not think or act how we would. Our limited minds can only go so far!

Isaiah 55:8 For My thoughts are not your thoughts, neither are your ways My ways, says the Lord.

Many times when things or situations seem questionable, it's an opportunity to muster up our faith and put our trust in Him! We can say to ourselves, "Ok, this is one of those times when I can't figure out what's going on, but I will put my trust in you God, because you know what's best for me." Let us pray, "Your will be done, Lord, not mine."

Trust that His ways are right, good and prosperous, looking out for our best interests. Let us put aside our stubbornness and yield to God's best for us! By submitting to His ways, you will be left with astonishing joy.

Have a dutiful day!

Day 9
KEEP UP YOUR COURAGE

As time goes on, where are you at this time in your life? Would you say that you're at a good place right now or struggling through difficult, challenging times?

Ecclesiastes 3:1,4,11 To everything there is a season, and a time for every matter or purpose under heaven: A time to weep and a time to laugh, a time to mourn and a time to dance. He has made everything beautiful in its time.

If you are going through hard times right now, do not even think about giving up!

Galatians 6:9 And let us not lose heart and grow weary and faint in acting nobly and doing right, for in due time and at the appointed season we shall reap, if we do not loosen and relax our courage and faint.

Let us remember to keep up our courage and find strength in God!

Isaiah 40:29 He gives power to the faint and weary, and to him who has no might He increases strength (causing it to multiply and making it to abound).

When going through the season of difficulty, remember God's promise to make everything beautiful in its time! Meanwhile, ask God to show, teach and help you to obey His ways. His beauty will be worth the wait.

Have a courageous day!

Day 10
A MAGNIFICENT MASTER PLAN FOR YOU

Think about this for a moment: the person you are *today* is a result of all the experiences you have had in the *past*, good and bad. As we continue on our journey of life, you will find that God has an ultimate, sovereign, good plan designed just for you.

Romans 8:28 We are assured and know that (God being a partner in their labor) all things work together and are (fitting into a plan) for good to and for those who love God and are called according to (His) design and purpose.

I remembered a time when I had my whole house remodeled. Coming home from work one day, to my great surprise, our dear contractor had decided to give us a bonus "gift"! Walking in the front door, I saw the beginning work of a big crown molding on top of our hallway that stuck out like a sore thumb... in the middle of my house! I couldn't breathe for awhile and was in shock.

Later, I decided to trust him. He had a beautiful design in his mind already planned out for my house, which I just couldn't see at the moment. The process of remodeling can be very ugly, but when the house was finished, it was beyond magnificent. The end result was much more than I could have ever imagined.

I encourage you to confidently trust God in your life! He can take your mistakes and bad situations and turn them into miracles. He has a magnificent master plan for you, full of goodness and purpose.

Have a trusting day!

Day 11
TIME FOR A NEW HEART?

Is it time for you to have a new heart? Is anyone tired of how your heart has become? Has it become calloused and is now of stone? Have the issues of life eventually gotten a hold of it? Does the thought of a new heart refresh you in any way?

Ezekiel 36:26 I will give you a new heart and put a new spirit in you; I will remove from you your heart of stone and give you a heart of flesh. And I will put my Spirit in you and move you to follow my decrees and be careful to keep my laws.

God has fulfilled His promise to us through Jesus' death and resurrection of giving us a new heart - the Holy Spirit now lives inside of us! With that act, we are able to walk in His ways and be rejuvenated to do His will.

Hebrews 13:21 Strengthen (complete, perfect) and make you what you ought to be and equip you with everything good that you may carry out His will; (while He Himself) works in you and accomplishes that which is pleasing in His sight, through Jesus Christ; to Whom be the glory forever.

With a new heart and spirit, let us be pleasing in God's sight, and have a heart that guarantees a blessed life.

Have a happy day!

Day 12
YOUR TRUE WORTH AND VALUE

Did you know that we stand out as a great treasure and value to God?

Matthew 10:29-31 Are not two little sparrows sold for a penny? And yet not one of them will fall to the ground without your Father's leave and notice. But even the very hairs of your head are all numbered. Fear not, then; You are of more value than many sparrows.

Can you just imagine that our Almighty God knows the intricate details of you and your life, up to the number of hairs you have each day. He notices everything about you and He'll always take care of you.

Exodus 19:5 Now therefore, if you will obey My voice in truth and keep My covenant, then you shall be My own peculiar possession and treasure from among and above all peoples; for all the earth is Mine.

Wow! To be God's very own peculiar possession and treasure, your true worth and value is a high priority in God's eyes. Let us obey His teachings and commands and honor Him in every way.

Have a significant day!

Day 13
ONE STEP AT A TIME

Are you familiar with the game in which you are blindfolded while another person takes your hand and leads you to a certain direction? Imagine the trust level you would need to have in order to take one step at a time with your guide! It can be a frightening thought. God wants our complete trust in Him. He is the guide in our lives! Sometimes we may want a blueprint for our lives or expect immediate answers, but we must develop patience and wait and trust in our loving God for everything.

Psalm 37:23-24 The steps of a (good) man are directed and established by the Lord when He delights in his way (and He busies Himself with his every step). Though he falls, he shall not be utterly cast down, for the Lord grasps his hand in support and upholds him.

What comfort it is to know that God is right there beside us, ready to grasp our hand and help us when we fall. With faith, let us take one step at a time in obedience to God, trusting that He has a good plan for our lives.

Isaiah 48:17 This is what the Lord says - your Redeemer, the Holy One of Israel; "I am the Lord your God, who teaches you what is best for you, who directs you in the way you should go.

He wants nothing but good for you!

Have an abiding day!

Day 14
FEEL YOUR FEAR, BUT CHOOSE TO FACE IT

Fear is a paralyzing feeling that won't go away until we confront it head on, and literally kill it! God says, "Fear not, for I am with you!" Facing the unknown can be frightening, but we must have faith and trust in God's promises to us.

Romans 8:15   For (the Spirit which) you have now received (is) not a spirit of slavery to put you once more in bondage to fear, but you have received the Spirit of adoption (the Spirit producing son ship) in (the bliss of) which we cry, Abba (Father)! Father!

As believers, we have God's Spirit within us! We must muster up all our fierceness from within and face our fear with the feeling of being afraid, but do it anyway!

One day I saw a gigantic water bug in the middle of our living room rug; it was humongous! I was alone and freaked out when I saw it, but I knew right then and there that I had to kill it. If I didn't, then it would eventually crawl around my house somewhere hiding and it would make me very uneasy knowing that it was around. So, I chose to face up to this gigantic bug and kill it! I got a big telephone book and ran up to it and tried to smack it down. It didn't work so I tried again and the third time around, I killed it! That experience was not fun at all, but it was worth it to try to attempt facing up to my fear of that bug and conquering my horrible feelings by killing it. Hooray! What a relief.

Let us pray that God will give us the same courage to confront our fears and conquer them with His Spirit!

Have a victoriously peaceful day!

Day 15
POWER OF THOUGHTS AND PERCEPTIONS

Did you know that who we are can be made up by our beliefs and perceptions? How we think and believe about ourselves has a great effect on our future.

Proverbs 23:7 For as he thinks in his heart, so is he.

It is very important not to allow ourselves to listen to the lies of the enemy through negative remarks from others, or seemingly negative circumstances that occur in our lives. We must train ourselves to be positive and listen only to the voice of God and His word of truth. If you want your life to change for the good, start today by filling yourself with good thoughts, knowing who you are in Christ and having His power within you.

Philippians 4:13 I have strength for all things in Christ Who empowers me.

Let us choose not to be like the cute but very sad character Eeyore from Winnie the Pooh, who always seems to have a dark cloud hovering over him. Instead, choose to break through the depression or any kind of negativity and be the bright light God desires for us to be in and through Him! He has a wonderful, good plan for our lives. Let us take Him up on the offer and choose to thrive; we'll have greater freedom, wholeness, and victory starting by the power of our thoughts!

Have a right-thinking day!

Day 16
KEEP MOVING FORWARD

Do you ever feel stuck or that you're moving backwards in life? How in the world can we change from our old, wrong behavior to a new, good and right one? Sometimes we may think it impossible to change or stop acting improperly. We beat ourselves up and get disappointed with ourselves and let others down as well.

Ephesians 4:22-24   You were taught, with regard to your former way of life, to put off your old self, which is being corrupted by its deceitful desires; to be made new in the attitude of your minds; and to put on the new self, created to be like God in true righteousness and holiness.

It starts with our minds. The way we think, our perspectives and attitudes, makes all the difference in the world. Once your outlook changes, your actions and behaviors will follow suit. If you purposely renew your mind in line with God's word and as we draw closer to Him, with the help of the Holy Spirit, we can actively start to strip off the layers of ugliness within us. By staying on the right path in God, and constantly renewing the spirit of our minds, good actions and behaviors will follow. Let's not stay content with where we are at, but keep moving forward and progress. Let's experience the good life God intended for us. His blessings of abundant life await us. I encourage you to have right thoughts that lead to right actions.

Have a good thinking day!

Day 17
DON'T JUMP THE GUN AND WORRY

Why jump the gun and worry about things that haven't happened yet?

Matthew 6:34 So do not worry or be anxious about tomorrow, for tomorrow will have worries and anxieties of its own. Sufficient for each day is its own trouble.

Isn't it amazing how one good phone call can change everything? Or perhaps a certain conversation with a person in conflict can result in something positive. When you perceive things in a different light and manner, it can change the way you look at them. As you do, your worries diminish and peace enters.

Let us choose not to worry but to live with peace and joy, meeting each day's challenges as they come. Know that God's grace and favor will be available sufficiently when we need it. Learn to live one day at a time, remembering God is always with us. Let us build our faith and trust in God's truth. His promises to care and provide for us are all that we need!

Let us not waste our precious energy drowning in our worries, but instead look up to God by fixing our eyes and being focused on Him. Trust that His mightiness, strength, protection and power will come through for you each day!

Have a worry-free day!

Day 18
THE KEY TO A POWERFUL AND JOYFUL LIFE

Is anyone interested in a powerful and joyful life? Here's the key!

Psalm 100:1-5 Shout for joy to the Lord, all the earth. Worship the Lord with gladness; come before Him with joyful songs. Know that the Lord is God. It is He who made us, and we are His; we are His people, the sheep of His pasture. Enter His gates with thanksgiving and His courts with praise; give thanks to Him and praise His name. For the Lord is good and His love endures forever; His faithfulness continues through all generations.

Thank goodness the Lord is good all the time and that He doesn't give us His mercy and kindness only when He feels like it. Let's be grateful that His faithfulness and truth are not limited, but endure forever! Having a heart of gratitude and praise all day long is where you find joy. If there is something that upsets you, right away think about something to be thankful about. There is great power in being joyful. Do not allow the enemy to steal it away from you.

2 Thessalonians 5:16-18 Be joyful always; pray continually; give thanks in all circumstances, for this is God's will for you in Christ Jesus.

We cannot go wrong with always having a thankful heart and partaking in God's will for us! Let us be encouraged to take hold of our powerful and joyful life.

Have an astounding day!

Day 19
HAVE YOU BECOME JADED?

Are we all familiar with the word *jaded*? It seems to describe something of a negative nature that happens over and over again until we eventually become numb to it. Notice how a clean object can be impacted by one tiny speck of dirt, but as the dirt accumulates through time, it becomes unnoticeable due to being jaded to the situation. That is how our hearts and lives can be. We sometimes may not realize the ugliness and filthiness around us because our hearts and minds have become corrupted by the evil around us. Be aware and very careful to keep your hearts clean!

Titus 1:15 Everything is pure to those whose hearts are pure. But nothing is pure to those who are corrupt and unbelieving, because their minds and consciences are corrupted.

Let us take inventory on our hearts and clean out all the junk. Pray for the Spirit to lead and guide you, so that we can walk in a right path with God and live a blameless life for Him! Always be encouraged to have a pure heart, seeking God and delighting in His presence, trusting and following His ways. Be kind and good to others! Immense blessings will come your way.

Have a clean hearted day!

Day 20
WHAT'S YOUR PURPOSE IN YOUR GENERATION?

Hopefully, there will come a time when we have our defining moment in our life, when we first come to the acknowledgement and realization that God alone is holy. Your life will have new direction and motivation. Your daily lives should reflect God's holiness. We need to have the defining moment of being cleansed, first and foremost, before we can clearly hear what God has called us to do, by His word, confirmation, and peace.

Isaiah 6:7-8 And with it he touched my mouth and said, Behold, this has touched your lips; your iniquity and guilt are taken away, and your sin is completely atoned for and forgiven. Also I heard the voice of the Lord, saying, Whom shall I send? And who will go for Us? Then said I, Here I am; send me.

God is looking for a person with a humble and willing heart to serve and be used by Him. Therefore, let us remember that God has made us perfect in Christ. He cleansed us first so that He could use us. Allow God to work in your life. Have a sense of passion and purpose being used by God in your own generation. Leave a legacy of God's influence everywhere!

Acts13:36 For David, after he had served God's will and purpose and counsel in his own generation, fell asleep.

Having the words spoken by God, "Well done, my good and faithful servant," is absolutely priceless.

Matthew 25:23 His master replied, well done, good and faithful servant! You have been faithful with a few

things; I will put you in charge of many things. Come and share your master's happiness!

Oh, such words! I encourage you to have that vision.

Have a meaningful day!

Day 21
BEWARE OF DECEPTION

When being deceived, we are tricked and blinded into believing in something we thought was true. The enemy is the ultimate master of lies! He twists the truth and lures us away from God, resulting in misery. Nothing is new with his ways and schemes. He is always up to his old tricks! Beware of deceptions!

John 8:44 He was a murderer from the beginning, not holding on to the truth, for there is not truth in him. When he lies, he speaks his native language, for he is a liar and the father of lies.

If you desire to have truth and freedom from within, I encourage you to know Christ and follow His ways!

John 8:32 And you will know the truth, and the truth will set you free.

Galatians 5:1 It is for freedom that Christ has set us free. Stand firm, then, and do not let yourselves be burdened again by a yoke of slavery.

I pray that if you are in any kind of bondage of sin or living a life of deception, you will be encouraged to choose freedom in Christ and know you belong to Him! Embrace God's word and know of His ways so that you can be on guard and not listen to the enemy's lies. The more truth you know, you'll be able to detect a lie. We are more than conquerors in Christ with His strength.

Have a conquering day!

Day 22
THE "MORE" FACTOR OF GREED

Greed can lead us into trouble when not in check! When we go to a buffet restaurant having all our favorite foods in sight, this can be a great challenge. Trying to limit our food intake on our plates, the uncontrollable "more factor" kicks in! What happens? We want more! The sight, smell and taste are ever so inviting! We desire more, without knowing that the more we get, real satisfaction cannot be reached to fulfill the void inside. That's how greed is. We can be so consumed and obsessed with wanting more money, power, possessions, prestige, beauty, and coveting our neighbor's things, never reaching the true deep peace and contentment.

1 Timothy 6:6-7 (And it is, indeed, a source of immense profit, for) godliness accompanied with contentment is great and abundant gain. For we brought nothing into the world, and obviously we cannot take anything out of the world.

Learning to be content is a never ending process, but once found, true peace, happiness, and contentment in one's life is evident!

Philippians 4:11-12 I am not saying this because I am in need, for I have learned to be content whatever the circumstances. I know what it is to be in need, and I know what it is to have plenty. I have learned the secret of being content in any and every situation, whether well fed or hungry, whether living in plenty or in want.

The simple life of contentment is where true peace is to be found!

Have a satisfied day!

Day 23
GREAT IS THY FAITHFULNESS

God is faithful. As the hymnal song reminds us, from *Great is Thy Faithfulness*, God is definitely the one and only person we can rely and depend on, and trust and confide in. He is consistent and never changing. He never leaves nor fails us in any way. He'll always provide all that we need. He offers peace by His presence to comfort, cheer, and guide. He gives us strength for today and bright hope for tomorrow. He gives us His blessings and much more is to come. What a glorious song. I encourage you to know and sing that song everyday and give Him praise.

Psalm 57:7-11 My heart is fixed, O God, my heart is steadfast and confident! I will sing and make melody. Awake, my glory (my inner self); awake, harp and lyre! I will awake right early. I will praise and give thanks to you, O Lord, among the peoples; I will sing praises to You among the nations. For Your mercy and loving kindness are great, reaching to the heavens, and Your truth and faithfulness to the clouds. Be exalted, O God, above the heavens; let your glory be over all the earth.

Seeing, hearing and experiencing God's glory and miracles, big or small, will make your heart sing and give Him praise. Let us have hearts that is beyond confident in God's faithfulness.

Have a magnificent day!

Day 24
CHOOSE THE RADIANCE OF LIFE

Are you interested in looking young, full of light, and radiant? Choose to follow Jesus and stay on His path which will give you light and lead you to life everlasting and joy.

John 8:12 Once more Jesus addresses the crowd. He said, I am the Light of the world. He who follows me will not be walking in the dark, but will have the Light which is Life.

By choosing Jesus in our hearts, the Holy Spirit fills us up.

John 7:38 He who believes in me (who cleaves to and trusts in and relies on Me) as the scripture has said, From his innermost being shall flow (continuously) springs and rivers of living water. But He was speaking here of the Spirit.

Let the Spirit of living water flow continuously in and through you. The look of freedom on one's face is beautiful and full of light and life. Living in darkness ages you; distress is written all over your face.

John 8:32 And you will know the Truth, and the Truth will set you free.

I pray as we choose the right path of God in our lives, your bondage will be broken by God's redeeming love and grace and His power will give you truth, light, freedom, and life. Your beauty will shine for years to come!

Have a beautiful day!

Day 25
DECISIONS? LET PEACE BE YOUR UMPIRE

Have you ever had an unsettling feeling inside your mind, unable to figure out why you feel heavy laden or overburdened with anxiety? God tells us to let peace rule in our hearts and allow it to be an umpire on all our decisions in life. When we don't know which way to go in our thoughts, actions, dealing with conflicts, raising children, etc., wait on God and be led by His peace to guide and direct you!

Colossians 3:15 And let the peace (soul harmony which comes) from Christ rule (act as umpire continually) in your hearts (deciding and settling with finality all questions that arises in your minds, in that peaceful state) to which as (members of Christ's) one body you were also called (to live). And be thankful (appreciative), (giving praise to God always).

Sometimes with our impatience, we act quickly on certain matters without regarding where God may be leading us. The results are usually frustrations, regrets and sorrow. Blessings come from our obedience in seeking God's peace. The umpire of peace will let you know if certain things should be in or out of your life. When questions arise, wait on God, and expect his peace to lead and guide you. Serenity will enter knowing you did God's will!

Have a yielding day!

Day 26
GOD SURELY DOES PROVIDE

Who me? Question Almighty God when in doubt? Where is my next meal coming from? How am I ever going to pay for this? It's amazing what happens when we put our trust in man, rather than on God. All kinds of fears creep in and take hold of us in very unhealthy ways. By putting God first and focusing on Him, our worries and anxieties seems to diminish and we feel a sense of comfort and great peace.

Hebrews 13:5 Let your character or moral disposition be free from love of money (including greed, avarice, lust, and craving for earthly possessions) and be satisfied with your present (circumstances and with what you have); for He (God) Himself has said, I will not in any way fail you nor give you up nor leave you without support. (I will) not, (I will) not, (I will) not in any degree leave you helpless nor forsake nor let (you) down (relax My Hold on you)! (Assuredly Not!)

Look where you are today. You are healthy, have clothes to wear and a roof over your head. God has provided for you in the past and surely will provide for your future. Build your trust and faith in Him to provide all that you need. Hold onto God's promises and faithfulness. Let Him amaze you with His providence. Don't question Him with *when*, *where*, and *how*, but simply pray and have faith. Wisely do your part and in His time, He will provide. Keep on trusting Him! Let Him do the work as it deepens our love and faith in Him.

Have a faithful day!

Day 27
OUR GOD, JEALOUS?

Isn't it kind of odd to think of our God as a jealous God? He wants to be the number one in our lives and for us to give Him our full attention.

James 4:5 Or do you suppose that the Scripture is speaking to no purpose that says, The Spirit Whom He has caused to dwell in us yearns over us and He yearns for the Spirit (to be welcome) with a jealous love?

Don't be surprised if God feels jealous when we may give more attention and time to our friends, job, money, possessions, own self sufficiency, etc.. He just may remove them from us for our own good! He wants to remind us that He is our first love, and for us to embrace fellowship with Him in His Spirit! Be aware of any distractions that may come before God. His love for you is so great that He actually gets jealous! Imagine that!

Exodus 20:3 You shall have no other gods before or besides Me.

His first commandment is given to us seriously, and we therefore we should take it with all seriousness! Let's keep Him first and foremost place in our lives and heart.

Have an attentive day!

Day 28
A VOID ONLY GOD CAN FILL UP

Are you feeling a little hungry these days? Are you pretty full? Do you even realize that you may be hungry? I hope you are not starved. How is your spiritual soul doing?

Psalm 107:9 For He satisfies the longing soul and fills the hungry soul with good.

Can you imagine our one and only being, Almighty God, is able to fill and completely satisfy to the fullest, your soul? Giving God priority in your life helps feed your hungry soul. We should seek Him with all our hearts, diligently with eagerness and enthusiasm.

Do you feel that you may have a void in your life? God is the only one that can satisfy your soul to the fullest. Nothing else works so go to Him. People try all kinds of other ways, means and methods to fill it up, but come to realize at sometime that they are not completely satisfied. Why? Because God meant for only Himself to be able to satisfy you completely in every way. Being hungry for God in your life is a good thing, for He fills you up with nothing but good.

Let us invest our time and efforts wisely, seeking Him for good nourishment and ultimate satisfaction. You will experience a satisfaction like you never have before.

Have a fulfilling day!

Day 29
GOOD HABITS ALWAYS WIN

They say it takes around 30 days to develop a habit! Unconsciously or consciously we can develop good or bad habits by repeating them daily.

Romans 2:8 But glory and honor and (heart) peace shall be awarded to everyone who (habitually) does good.

Did you hear that? If you desire inner peace, magnificent glory and honor, then all you have to do is consciously develop good habits! Good habits in anything will be beneficial for your health, mind and soul; kind words, helping others, consistently and patiently being persistent in anything good.

Romans 2:7 To those who by patient persistence in well doing seek (unseen but sure) glory and honor and (the eternal blessedness of) immorality, He will give eternal life.

Developing good habits are definitely a win-win situation in all areas of your life! I challenge you to make good choices, keep on making good choices, and see what happens. By reading my daily encouragements, you have developed a good habit of reading God's word daily. Keep on keeping on!

Have a rewarding day!

Day 30
FEAR ONLY GOD

Did you know that you are offending God when you have and give into your fears -- fears of any kind. When we have fears, it's a normal reaction to things that can trigger us the wrong way. We can start to panic as our anxiety rises. Fear is contagious. When others are in fear, it can rub off on us as well. We can eventually believe their fears. Don't allow that to happen nor should you be the cause of others to fear.

Isaiah 8:12-14   Do not call conspiracy all that this people will call conspiracy; neither be in fear of what they fear, nor (make others afraid and) in dread. The Lord of hosts -- regard Him as holy and honor His holy name (by regarding Him as your only hope of safety), and let Him be your fear and let Him be your dread (lest you offend Him by your fear of man and distrust of Him). And he shall be a sanctuary (a sacred and indestructible asylum to those who reverently fear and trust in Him).

To fear God is having reverential awe, respect, and knowledge that He is holy. He is the ultimate in taking away all of your fears. Trust and rely on Him and let Him be your refuge, shelter, and sanctuary. He has the power to do anything He wants for He created all the earth and everything in it. When in fear, know that He's right there with you and will help you through all your difficulties. He is your Prince of peace. I encourage you to give Him your fears and let Him take care of it. You will be in awe.

Have a peaceful day!

Day 31
WHO ME, JUDGE?

We all tend to judge people from their outward appearances. We just can't help it! But God judges according to the *heart*.

1 Samuel 16:7 But the Lord said to Samuel, Look not on his appearance or at the height of his statue, for I have rejected him. For the Lord sees not as man sees; for man looks on the outward appearance, but the Lord Looks on the heart.

Having a pure heart is vital. Get in touch with your inner lives and heart attitudes. Our motives, thoughts, and feelings need to be consistent with God's heart! Imagine the way we see ourselves may be completely different from how others see and judge us. I encourage you to put on God's glasses and try to see people through His eyes, beyond the outer appearance. It is possible to put up a good front and still have an impure heart, and vice versa. Work with the Holy Spirit to let the thoughts and attitudes of Jesus reside in you.

Philippians 2:5 Let this same attitude and purpose and (humble) mind be in you which was in Christ Jesus: (Let Him be your example in humility).

I encourage you to put more time and effort in your inner being, which counts, rather than the externals.

Have a kind day!

Day 32
FULLY BELIEVE GOD'S PROMISES WITHOUT A DOUBT

Have you ever believed in someone so much that you never doubted him? If he told you that he was going to do something, you would have no reason to doubt him. You would fully believe that it will happen. Promises made and kept are a treasure. As we empower our faith in God and praise and glorify Him in everything, we will have a deep sense within us, with full assured confidence that God is a man of His word and fully able to keep His promises.

Romans 4:20-21 Abraham never wavered in believing God's promise. In fact, his faith grew stronger, and in this he brought glory to God. He was fully convinced that God is able to do whatever He promises.

God does not waver when He speaks. He means what He says and promises to fulfill them to the end. As God as our example, let us follow through with our spoken words of promise to others. When it comes to God, do not have a flicker of doubt in you. He wants to see our trust and faith in Him. He is actively working on His promises to you. It may be discreet or obvious, but know that it is happening. He won't let you down. Keep your faith active, alive, and energized.

Have a promising day!

Day 33
SPEAK POSITIVE WORDS OF FAITH INTO YOUR FUTURE

There is a lot of power in what we think and say about ourselves, and that affects our future. Notice when people keep saying positive or negative words all the time, you end up producing just that! If you feel defeated all the time and nothing seems to go right, don't be surprised if miserable and bad things seem to happen only to you! On the other hand if we constantly say positive, victorious words, we move toward that incredible power that leads us to victory!

Mark 5:28-29 For she kept saying, if I only touch His garments, I shall be restored to health. And immediately her flow of blood was dried up at the source, and (suddenly) she felt in her body that she was healed of her (distressing) ailment.

Pay attention to what you're saying about yourself and for your future. Dr. Wayne Dyer said "Happiness is something you decide ahead of time! When you change the way you look at things, the things you look at change. Connect with God, He is our source!"

I encourage you to think and say good, positive, victorious words! Get rid of the word "defeat" from your mind. Train yourself daily to speak positive words in faith.

Have a victorious day!

Day 34
START TO SPEAK GOD'S WORD FOR SUCCESS

How in the world are we to rise above situations that seem very difficult for us to handle? When you speak God's word and His favor at your difficulties and obstacles, you will defeat them and turn them into success. God's Spirit and His power go to work on your behalf of your faith.

Joshua 1:8 This Book of the Law shall not depart out of your mouth, but you shall meditate on it day and night, that you may observe and do according to all that is written in it. For then you shall make your way prosperous, and then you shall deal wisely and have good success.

Obstacles are never permanent. Take action, meditate and speak God's word at your troubles day and night for victory. The word is your sword which has great power. Keep them in the center of your heart, for they bring life and health to your mind, body, and soul.

Proverbs 4:20-22 My son, attend to my words; consent and submit to my sayings. Let them not depart from your sight; keep them in the center of your heart. For they are life to those who find them, healing and health to all their flesh.

When you fill your mind with God's word, you'll have truth, freedom, victory, and peace. I encourage you and dare you to think and speak God's word in faith at your troubles.

Have a conquering day!

Day 35
JESUS WAS EMOTIONALLY DISTRESSED, YET CHOSE TO OBEY GOD

If a dearly loved person asked you to do something that was painful, challenging, and sacrificial, would you do it? Has your soul ever been distressed and deeply troubled? Jesus has too. He knew that God wanted Him to die on the cross for us. Thank goodness He willingly obeyed so that we could be saved from our sins and have everlasting life. Imagine, though, if He disobeyed out of anguish!

Mark 14:32-36 They went to a place called Gethsemane, and Jesus said to his disciples, Sit here while I pray. He took Peter, James and John along with him, and he began to be deeply distressed and troubled. My soul is overwhelmed with sorrow to the point of death. Going a little farther, he fell to the ground and prayed that if possible the hour might pass from him. "Abba, Father," he said, "everything is possible for you. Take this cup from me, yet not what I will, but what you will."

What a great example He was. Our emotions are fickle and can get us into trouble. Learn how to control them and yield to the Holy Spirit, our helper, to do what is right. Remember who and whose you are -- a child of God. You have God's power and strength alive in your Spirit to help you and to obey God and do what is right. Learn to make decisions based on what we know, rather than on how we feel. Rewards will be blessings and abundant life.

Have a yielding day!

Day 36
DISTRACTIONS AND DISRUPTIONS BE GONE

You may think that you are doing just fine and dandy with the direction that your life, and your spiritual life with God, is going. Then all of the sudden a disruption or distraction to go in the wrong direction may abruptly enter! What do you do?

Proverbs 4:25-27   Let your eyes look right on (with fixed purpose), and let your gaze be straight before you. Consider well the path of your feet, and let all your ways be established and ordered a right. Turn not aside to the right hand or to the left; remove your foot from evil.

Be sensitive to the Spirit's leading.

Proverbs 14:15-16   A simple man believes everything, but a prudent man gives thoughts to his steps. A wise man fears the Lord and shuns evil, but a fool is hotheaded and reckless.

Let us be aware, watchful, and prepared on the direction you are going! When evil strikes, take it as a red light warning and don't go in that direction! Immediately refocus and fix your eyes straight ahead on the right course for your life. It's a guarantee that many distractions will come; the question is, how are we to respond to them? I pray that by first fearing the Lord, we will give wise thoughts to our steps!

Have a watchful day!

Day 37
EXPECT GOD'S GOODNESS

Have you ever experienced that wonderful anticipation that something good is going to happen, that you will get that promotion, or receive an awesome gift of some kind, or things may go your way? All we have to do on our part is to wait, hope, and expect it to happen. God wants us to have that kind of expectation from Him.

Psalm 27:13-14 I am still confident of this: I will see the goodness of the Lord in the land of the living. Wait for the Lord; be strong and take heart and wait for the Lord.

God cannot wait to give us all of His goodness. While we wait, he wants us to be brave, in whatever hopeless situation or trying times you might face, and have the courage and endurance, to keep on keeping on and stay focused on Him. Something good is surely to happen! Meanwhile, have the patience and a hopeful heart to never give up and expect God's goodness of His victory and His favor in every way. He can and will give you His love, joy, peace, and many blessings as you stay in faith and believe. It will definitely be worth the wait.

Have a joyfully expectant day!

Day 38
PROCLAIM YOUR PEACE

One of God's many wonderful promises to us is that He gives us His peace but it's our job to pursue it, guard it, activate it, and proclaim it. Say to yourself, "Peace is mine." Don't give into your flesh and all of its unhealthy ways.

John 14:27 Peace I leave with you; my (own) peace I now give and bequeath to you. Not as the world gives do I give to you. Do not let your hearts be troubled, neither let them be afraid, stop allowing yourselves to be agitated and disturbed; and do not permit yourselves to be fearful and intimidated and cowardly and unsettled.

Living in God's peace and in His spirit is where you want to be. That is truly a blessed life. God's peace is already within you. Let us pursue it and be lead by it every day as we praise God for it. The more you learn to access your peace, your fleshy ways diminishes. Don't allow frustrations and fears to take over. Each day, let us tap into our peace given to us from God and let it take place and reside in our hearts. Proclaim your peace and take ownership of it.

Have the most peaceful day!

Day 39
BE AWARE OF H.A.L.T., WHICH LEADS TO SIN

There is a way which sin and temptation can get a hold on you! Pastor Charles Stanley talks about H.A.L.T.: Don't allow yourself to get too **Hungry, Angry, Lonely,** and **Tired.** When you allow yourself to be in the position of all four ingredients, the opportunity of sin can be inviting.

Romans 7:8 But sin, finding opportunity in the commandment (to express itself), got a hold on me and aroused and stimulated all kind of forbidden desires (lust, covetousness). For without the law sin is dead.

Do not take advantage of sin because we live in God's mercy and favor.

Romans 6:22 But now since you have been set free from sin and have become the slaves of God, you have your present reward in holiness and its end is eternal life.

Choose to surrender to God and pray for His strength, mercy, grace, wisdom, and discernment. I encourage you to keep yourself in check and stay on the path of righteousness that leads to eternal life. Be alert and aware of your positions to develop good habits of a healthy balance in your life!

Have a discerning day!

Day 40
GOD'S ZEAL FOR YOUR LIFE

We all have our own paths and races in our lives set before us. It is up to us to be responsible for our own personal relationships with God, to carry out His good works with zeal and enthusiasm.

Philippians 2:12-13 Therefore, my dear ones, as you have always obeyed, so now, not only in my presence but much more because I am absent, work out (cultivate, carry out to the goal, and fully complete) your own salvation with reverence and awe and trembling (self-distrust, with serious caution, tenderness of conscience, watchful against temptation, timidly shrinking from whatever might offend God and discredit the name of Christ). (Not in your own strength) for it is God Who is all the while effectually at work in you (energizing and creating in you the power and desire), both to will and work for His good pleasure and satisfaction and delight.

No need to worry for God gives us His strength which effectively works in us with His delight as we do God's will in our lives. Yield to His Spirit everyday and watch what God will do to you, in you, and through you. You will be in awe. Run your own race with all of your diligence and enthusiasm, and God's strength and power to carry out His will and receive your crown of glory.

Have a triumphant day!

Day 41
FORGIVENESS IS THE BEGINNING TO OUR HEALING

Why is it so hard to simply *forgive* someone that has hurt us? We hold on to resentment, which is very unhealthy for our heart and soul! We just don't seem to understand the people that hurt us, and we choose to stay ignorant to why they do what they do.

Well, forgiveness is the beginning to our healing! We must learn to even forgive ourselves from past mistakes, giving them to God and moving on with the wonderful life God has in stored for us.

Matthew 6:14   For if you forgive men when they sin against you, your heavenly father will also forgive you. But if you do not forgive men their sins, your Father will not forgive your sins.

Forgiveness is serious business! We are the ones who get hurt if we do not forgive. Jesus made it plain and simple to forgive not just once, but seventy times seven!

Matthew 18:21-23   Then Peter came up to Him and said, Lord, how many times may my brother sin against me and I forgive him and let it go? (As many as) up to seven times? Jesus answered him, I tell you, not up to seven times, but seventy times seven!

God knows that we are human and continue making mistakes in our lives. We are all broken people and we need Jesus' love and forgiveness. As Jesus was hanging on the cross, he prayed to God to forgive the people for they do not know what they are doing. Jesus was the perfect example of forgiveness, from being ridiculed, beaten, misjudged, hated etc., to *choosing* to die for us and forgive despite the ugliness people had shown him. His love was greater and His love covered all sins.

Let us be encouraged to forgive as Jesus forgave, to start our healing process in every area of our lives! By forgiving, you will definitely do yourselves a great favor of opening doors to restoration and blessings galore! Ask God to help you forgive as you have been forgiven. Let us live the good life that God has given freely in peace and in harmony.

Have a blessed day!

Day 42
YOUR HERO AND PROTECTOR

How would you like to have your very own personal bodyguard? God is our personal protector from all evil. He shields us emotionally, physically, and spiritually with His protective power for His sovereign plan in our lives. However, His protection is sometimes unrecognizable. It can come in many different forms. It can be obvious, painful, or challenging but they are His ways of protection.

Psalm121:7-8 The Lord will keep you from all evil; He will keep your life. The Lord will keep your going out and your coming in from this time forth and forevermore.

He is always watching over us with His attentive eyes, never losing sight of where we are at in our lives. He doesn't want harm to come to us so focus on Him and allow Him to direct your ways.

Proverb 2-8 That he may guard the paths of justice; yes, He preserves the way of His saints.

Can you imagine your life without God's protection? Where would we be now?

Psalm 66: 8-9 Bless our God, O peoples, give Him grateful thanks and make the voice of His praise be heard. Who put and kept us among the living, and has not allowed our feet to slip.

Thank God continually for being our hero and for His marvelous protection.

Have a secured day!

Day 43
MY PERSONAL COUNSELOR

Can you imagine having your very own free, lifetime, personal counselor?

Psalm 32:8 I (the Lord) will instruct you and teach you in the way you should go; I will counsel you with my eye upon you.

How comforting is that? God's word is a powerful source of guidance and truth. We develop a deep, personal knowledge of God through His word. John Macarthur tells us "How to study the bible" by the steps of: believe it, honor, love, and fight for it, obey, preach and study it. With that, God has given us the Holy Spirit to lead and guide us in the right direction of our lives. Do not resist the Spirit's promptings, but be willing to follow it.

Proverbs 1:5 The wise also will hear and increase in learning, and the person of understanding will acquire skill and attain to sound counsel (so that he may be able to steer his course rightly).

Wisdom starts with reverential fear and awe of God. I pray you will be wise to accept God as your counselor and to lean on His truth, wisdom, and guidance accompanied by His Spirit. His ways will lead you to everlasting peace, joy, and an abundant life.

Have an accepting day!

Day 44
WHAT IS GOD'S COMMAND TO YOU

Take a moment and think of the word *command*. It is not a suggestion, "maybe", or "if." It is a direct order from God to us.

Joshua 1:9 Have I not commanded you? Be strong, vigorous, and very courageous. Be not afraid, neither be dismayed, for the Lord your God is with you wherever you go.

Do not shrink back in fear and worries. Do not allow it to take over your mind, will or abilities. It is a natural tendency to react in fear when certain unknown, challenging or frightening things happen to us. We need to take the steps of faith to be bold and courageous with the guaranty of the Almighty God on our side! We do not necessarily need to know how, when or what God is going to do to help us. We only need to trust and know He is always with us and will never leave or forsake us.

When God asks you to do something, don't make excuses and look to yourself or others. Only look to God! Don't look at the circumstances or other people's reactions, etc... Just remember that God is with you and that is all you need. I encourage you to face whatever fears you may have and obey God and "Do it afraid." Put your feelings and emotions aside and obediently take action. God is with you every step of the way to help you conquer and have victory. He is our source of peace.

Have a courageous day!

Day 45
WHERE'S YOUR JOY?

Have you ever had one of those days where everything seemed to go wrong? Have you ever felt down or angry even when things around you were good? Maybe you can search deeper within you and find the source of this negativity.

Psalm51:10-12 Create in me a clean heart, O God, and renew a right, persevering, and steadfast spirit within me. Cast me not away from your presence and take not your Holy Spirit from me. Restore to me the joy of Your salvation and uphold me with a willing spirit.

The main ingredient lacking in your life was joy. You find joy in God's presence. When He is not near and dear to your heart, something is missing and things easily bother us.

Nehemiah 8:10 And be not grieved and depressed, for the joy of the Lord is your strength and stronghold.

Whenever you feel weak, depressed or defeated, remember the power of joy in the Lord. That's where you find your strength. Having a heart of thankfulness always allows God to be in your presence which gives you joy. Cultivate and practice it daily and be a blessing to others. Your spirit will soon be renewed, rejuvenated and full of life and joy.

Have a renewed joyous day!

Day 46
HOPE AS OUR ANCHOR

If we were to put our hope in someone, who would it be? How about putting our hope into someone who is steadfast, never changing, guarantees His promises and who is always faithful? How does that sound?

Hebrews 6:17-19 Because God wanted to make the unchanging nature of his purpose very clear to the heirs of what was promised, he confirmed it with an oath. God did this so that, by two unchangeable things in which it is impossible with God to lie, we who have fled to take hold of the hope offered to us may be greatly encouraged. We have this hope as an anchor for the soul, firm and secure. It enters the inner sanctuary behind the curtain.

Thank goodness we have hope as our firm, immovable, steady strong anchor! Otherwise, we would be tossed around back and forth without any steadiness in our life. God is our rock and let us cling onto Him and hope in all His promises. When we only rely on ourselves, it can make the heart sick!

Proverbs 13:12 Hope deferred makes the heart sick, but when the desire is fulfilled, it is a tree of life...

As believers, we have a hope that anchors our souls and with that, we flourish into a tree of life. Always tap into your hope and pray for God's goodness.

Have a secured day!

TOUCH GOD'S HEART

Did you know, there is a way to bring joy and gladness to our God?

Proverbs 23:15-16 My child, if your heart is wise, My own heart will rejoice! Everything in me will celebrate when you speak what is right.

When we choose to speak what is right by having and developing a wise heart, we bring tears of joy to our own Almighty God. Imagine that! Let us be encouraged to have the desire to do good, cultivate a wise heart and speak whatever is true and right.

Philippians 4:8 And now, dear brothers and sisters, one final thing. Fix your thoughts on what is true, and honorable, and right, and pure, and lovely, and admirable. Think about things that are excellent and worthy of praise.

When we develop a wise heart and speak on what is right, which starts by having right thoughts, our words are precious gifts given to God. He rejoices and celebrates. Strengthening your own relationship with God by having wisdom and righteousness produces a wonderful, healthy and prosperous relationship with Him. Let us touch God's heart by making Him rejoice.

Have a wise day!

Day 48
HOW DO YOU VALUE YOUR TIME?

Have you ever thought to yourself that there is too much to do and such little time? God is telling us to value our time here on earth.

Ephesians 5:15-17 Be very careful, then, how you live- not as unwise but as wise, making the most of every opportunity, because the days are evil. Therefore do not be foolish, but understand what the Lord's will is.

Let us live purposefully and productively, being wise in the way you walk, deciding on what to do or not to do. Each day, pray for understanding on what your will may be for that day. As a parent, it can be on how to care for your child. At your work place it may be to be diligent and excellent in all that you do. In your friendships, it may be to be supportive and share in healthy good times. Let us have the growing awareness on prioritizing what is important and to balance out our schedules in a healthy and productive manner. Wasting time does not go well with God's plans for us. Live on purpose and pray that God will teach you to live wisely.

Have a productive day!

Day 49
JEALOUSY, IF NOT CHECKED, LEADS TO CRAZINESS

Are you familiar with the green-eyed monster named *jealousy*? Some of us may not like to admit that jealousy lies within. Let me warn you to be extremely careful with that emotion! It can start out subtle but if not in check, it can develop over time and feed off on all the ugly emotions that come with it: Selfishness, hatred, bitterness, resentment, anger, gossip, mental disturbances...

Proverbs 27:4 Wrath is fierce and anger is a flood, but who can stand before jealousy?

Jealousy is an uncontrollable emotion that can take over your mind, emotions, and your entire being. Do not take jealousy too lightly. Many people have had ruined and destroyed relationships due to jealousy! How very sad and unfortunate that they chose to let that get in the way of what God intended for us to have: walking in love and in harmony with one another. When you allow jealousy to feed off from itself, eventually you may become unrecognizable!

2 Corinthians 12:20 For I am afraid that perhaps when I come I may find you to be not that I wish and may be found by you to be not what you wish; that perhaps there will be strife, jealousy, angry tempers, disputes, slanders, gossip, arrogance, disturbances.

I encourage you to pray that with the Holy Spirit, He will help you to control and diminish your jealousy, so that you may be in your right mind when you meet Christ!

Have a clear thinking day!

Day 50
THE CHOICE TO LIVE IN PEACE

Is anyone in conflict, or perhaps disturbed and full of animosity? We should do our part to feel responsible to love and be at peace with one another. There is no greater place than to be in peace -- peace with difficult circumstances, peace with one another and peace with yourself.

2 Corinthians 13:11 Aim for perfection, listen to my appeal, be of one mind, live in peace. And the God of love and peace will be with you.

Our God of love will give us His peace as we are strengthened each day to learn, grow and be encouraged to live at peace with everyone around us. Things may never be resolved if we just wait around and do nothing. We should be proactive to be of the same agreeable mind with one another and to strive to live at peace. Then God says, He, being the source of affection, goodwill, love and peace, will be with you. How wonderful is that?

Have a wonderful day of serenity!

Day 51
LIES GET OUT! BE TRANSFORMED BY THE TRUTH

Lies, lies, lies, get out! It is the truth that transforms us! It is alive and sets us free! When God speaks into your heart, things change! Little by little you are in the process of transforming into the likeness of His Son Jesus.

Acts 20:32   God's...gracious Word can make you into what he wants you to be and give you everything you could possibly need.

We can find God's truth, answers, gifts, provisions, and transformations of building you up all in His word. Spiritual growth is the process of replacing lies with truth. If someone gave you counterfeit money, it would be very difficult to detect that it isn't real. It looks, feels, and seems real; only trained people will see the difference. Why? In this same way, we need to be trained in God's Word and mature in the Spirit to know the truth that will set us free. I encourage you to know and study God's truth, so that you may be able to detect a lie with the help of God's Spirit.

John 8:31   If you bide in My word (hold fast to My teachings and live in accordance with them), you are truly My disciples. And you will know the truth, and the truth will set you free.

Living a life filled with lies can be entrapping and blinding, Pray that God will help you know the truth which sets you free.

Have a freeing day!

Day 52
GOD DESERVES OUR PRAISE

What comes to your mind when you think about our Lord? He is everything that is good, spectacular, magnificent and glorious. In thinking and meditating on God, He wants and desires us to simply, praise Him.

Psalm 113:1-3 Praise the Lord! (Hallelujah!) Praise, O servants of the Lord, praise the name of the Lord! Blessed be the name of the Lord from this time forth and forever. From the rising of the sun to the going down of it and from east to west, the name of the Lord is to be praised!

From a.m. to p.m., now and forever, God wants our praise. Through our thoughts, actions, service, speech and our whole being, we should aim to naturally give Him praise in everything. He deserves our praise and yearns to hear from us. His main goal of creating us is to please and glorify Him in every manner of our lives. Let's be encouraged to make it a daily practice to praise our Lord.

Have a glorious day!

Day 53
WAIT ON GOD'S PERFECT TIMING

Isn't it amazing how time flies by so fast? Yet, we still want certain things to come quickly in this fast-paced world.

Try not to go with your own plans ahead of God's timing. You may not get the full benefit of what you hoped for or desired. Yield to the Holy Spirit to guide and direct you in the way you should go. Meanwhile, learn to have patience and wait hopefully and expectantly on God's divine timing! Then you will get your full reward and blessings.

This time in your life may or may not be the right season for certain requests, answers or breakthroughs, but when the right season comes, along comes God's abundant harvest and overflowing blessings. You will be in awe.

Ecclesiastes 3:11 He has made everything beautiful in its time.

I encourage you to hang in there and not to give up. Give God thanks as you patiently wait on His perfect time. The good things you believe in God for are on their way. Trust in Him and keep on trusting in Him!

Have an expectant, beautiful day!

Day 54
GOD FINISHES WHAT HE STARTS

Have you ever started on a task or project, never to finish it? Or, maybe you are working on one right now and are determined to work on it until the very end? God started a good work in you and promises to bring you to a full completion to the end.

Philippians 1:6 And I am convinced and sure of this very thing, that He Who began a good work in you will continue until the day of Jesus Christ (right up to the time of His return), developing (that good work) and perfecting and bringing it to full completion in you.

If you feel that you are being hard on yourself in any way or just want to give up, know that God doesn't give up on you. He knows we are a "work in progress" and will be for the rest of our lives. We are never perfect, but we are perfect in and through Christ. God is diligently working in us behind the scenes, developing that good work in us and bringing it to full completion. Be patient with yourselves as we trust in God's character, knowing that He always finishes what He starts. He will never quit and give up on you. Be encouraged to stay in faith, keeping your focus on Him and to keep on keeping on.

Have a promising day!

Day 55
YOUR TEARS ARE NOT WASTED

There are so many times we may feel alone, down and out, overwhelmed by complete sadness and that no one cares or listens to our cries. But behold, take heed with comfort, for our Loving, Compassionate God sees and hears every tear drop: they are not wasted!

Psalm 40:1 I waited patiently and expectantly for the Lord; and He inclined to me and heard my cry.

Through our sufferings, there is great hope!

1 Peter 5:10 And after you have suffered a little while, the God of all grace (Who imparts all blessings and favor), who has called you to His (own) eternal glory in Christ Jesus, will Himself complete and make you what you ought to be, establish and ground you securely, and strengthen and settle you.

He will help to bring you back to your feet and on stable ground!

1 John 5:14 And this is the confidence which we have in Him. (We are sure) that if we ask anything (make any request) according to His will (in agreement with His own plan), He listens to and hears us.

Take comfort in that! Let us be encouraged to hope in God's promises to us for they are real and alive. Reach out to God as He holds out His mighty hands and trust in His endearing, wonderful ways, for He loves and cares for us, His children, dearly!

Have a comforting day!

Day 56
WAIT, HOPE AND EXPECT

While we are living here in this present moment, we must believe in the Lord's goodness. If we are going through a difficult time in our lives, God wants us to wait for Him, keep our hope alive, and expect Him to be in our presence as we have all His goodness coming our way. We need to be brave and muster up all the courage from within knowing His goodness is coming.

Psalm 27:13-14 (What, what would have become of me) had I not believed that I would see the Lord's goodness in the land of the living! Wait and hope for and expect the Lord; be brace and of good courage and let your heart be stout and enduring. Yes, wait for and hope for and expect the Lord.

Don't give up! God wants us to experience His goodness. Stay in faith and pray for wisdom and guidance in all your matters. Know that He is working on your situation. As we endure and persevere through hard times, know it'll be worth the wait as we envelop all of God's blessings and promises.

Have a hopeful day!

Day 57
TRANSFORMED INTO A RENEWED MIND

In what state of mind shall we go into the New Year? How about being transformed into a new and improved you? Sounds good? It all starts with a renewed mindset.

Romans 12:2 Do not conform any longer to the pattern of this world, but be transformed by the renewing of your mind. Then you will be able to test and approve what God's will is – His good, pleasing and perfect will.

We all have the power to choose if we are going to be in the same old attitude, mindset and behaviors or to be transformed into a renewed mind!

Philippians 4:8 Whatever is true, worthy of reverence, just and pure, loveable, kind, winsome, gracious, if there is any virtue and excellence, anything worthy of praise, think on these things.

As we look into and recognize what is God's good will for us in the next year, let us embrace it and take it on with a fresh renewed mind and attitude. Studying and digging into God's word of truth is the key foundation to help you change your mind set to good thoughts! All of God's promises are in His word and He never breaks not even one of His promises to us! Holding onto God's truth always gives us hope and joy.

Have a renewed, thinking day!

Day 58
ROUGH TIMES

Is anyone going through a difficult time in their lives right now? It's important to get a clear perspective and view on such arduous matters. We can always assume the worst in everything. However, when we look deeper within for the cause and effect of things and are open to change for the better good, deeper and richer things can flourish. Certain things are worth looking into for the sake of a healthy mind, heart and also for building wonderful relationships.

Jeremiah 29:11 For I know the thoughts and plans I have for you, says the Lord, thoughts and plans for welfare and peace and not for evil, to give you hope in your final outcome.

When we build our faith in God, He makes good things come about from bad circumstances. Who knows what's in His plan, but it's our job to keep looking up and stay focused on Him as we trust in Him no matter what. The challenging times will eventually pass and lead us to victory as we keep our eyes fixed on God. I pray that you will have the patience and endurance to keep fighting the good fight. Don't allow the enemy to bring you down; stand firm on the Rock (our God and refuge) and remember who and to whom you belong. You are a child of God. Let's be encouraged to pray for God's breakthrough in His perfect timing!

Have a steadfast day!

Day 59
WHERE'S YOUR POISE AND CONFIDENCE?

Notice how we tend to cheer and focus on the confidence level of our children, friends, and loved ones. However, we should be careful on not putting too much confidence on the externals, for they can only be temporary! Let us put no confidence in ourselves, but rather have the right poise of Godly confidence!

Philippians 3:3 For we (Christians) are the true circumcision, who worship God in spirit and by the Spirit of God and exult and glory and pride ourselves in Jesus Christ, and put no confidence or dependence (on what we are) in the flesh and on outward privileges and physical advances and external appearances.

Anything can happen for us to lose fleshly things; that is why it is very important not to depend so much on them with all your confidence! Rather we should put our confidence in God, where it truly matters. He is the source of giving you all your abilities and beauty.

The late Coach John Wooden said, "Poise and confidence is just being yourself!" Don't compare with others. That's where we can get in trouble! Let us be confident on how God created us in His image, which is full of beauty and capability in Him alone! Let us put our confidence in His love and provisions for us and lean on Him for everything. Your poise matters to God and that's what truly counts!

Have a confident day in Christ!

Day 60
TAKE THE TIME TO LOOK DEEPER

How easy it is to judge a book by its cover, only to look at the surface and not take the time to look a little deeper. How deep are you willing to look into your challenges: a difficult person, a troublesome relationship, or trying issues that keep rising up?

Proverbs 20:5 Counsel in the heart of man is like water in a deep well, but a man of understanding draws it out.

Through the Holy Spirit, let us put the effort to draw out understanding from our well.

Proverbs 19:20 Hear counsel, receive instruction, and accept correction, that you may be wise in the time to come.

Let us always be reminded to take a step back from any hardship and not give in to automatically react. Following the wisdom of understanding ultimately brings us peace.

Let us be encouraged to draw out all of God's wisdom, discernment and counsel from deep within and have patience as we explore all of God's richness from what He is trying to teach us through it all.

Have a wise day!

Day 61
THE PRIORITY OF PLEASING GOD IN EVERYTHING

Have you ever been in a win-win situation? The results are the reward. What must we do to receive the reward of deeply knowing God and receiving his many blessings?

Colossians 1:10 That you may walk (live and conduct yourselves) in a manner worthy of the Lord, fully pleasing to Him and desiring to please Him in all things, bearing fruit in every good work and steadily growing and increasing in and by the knowledge of God (with fuller, deeper, and clearer insight, acquaintance, and recognition).

How do you desire to please someone if we don't know him, let alone, like him? God is inviting us to know Him and become acquainted with Him and to grow steadily knowing all that He is: our magnificent, glorious Almighty God. Ask God to fill you with the knowledge of His will and His spiritual wisdom so that you can live a fruitful life pleasing Him in all that you do. Pray that His power and might will help us along the way. As believers, God molds us into Christ's likeness so that we are a light reflecting God's glory to this world. As people notice and wonder where the source of your light is, it will be a wonderful opportunity to share the good news of Christ. It's a guarantee: His bountiful blessings come by our obedience to God and pleasing Him. So, grow in Christ and please Him in everything.

Have a focused day!

Day 62
IT'S A BIG DEAL

Doesn't it feel wonderful when you have worked hard on something worthwhile and you are acknowledged on your good works? People then say, "Good job. Well done," and "You deserved it." Yet, can you imagine getting that kind of praise from our Almighty God? How about on the little things you do which no one seems to notice? Be assured, God sees them all and greatly rewards you especially for the little things.

Matthew 25:21 His master said to him, Well done, you upright (honorable, admirable) and faithful servant! You have been faithful and trustworthy over a little; I will put you in charge of much. Enter into and share the joy (the delight, the blessedness) which your master enjoys.

God is so proud of us as we stay faithful in the little things. He then trusts us to be in charge of greater things. Although it may not be a big deal to us, it is a big deal in God's eyes. It means we have the potential and capacity to do much for His kingdom. Then we will rejoice together.

Have a purposeful day!

Day 63
THE EFFECTS OF YOUR DECISIONS

We can never go wrong with having reverential awe and fear for God. Doing what's right by keeping His commandments will get you far in life! Not only in your life, but your children's, grandchildren's, and so on. It's a wonder how we can pass down our behaviors, lifestyle and faith on to the next generations. When we come to the realization that we're living here on earth not only for ourselves but that we have an effect on others, we may stop and think twice on the choices and decisions we make!

Deuteronomy 5:29 Oh, that they had such a (mind and) heart in them always (reverently) to fear me and keep all My commandments, that it might go well with them and with their children forever!

Let's be that person whose life seems to go well by first fearing God and keeping His commands!

Deuteronomy 5:32-33 So be careful to do what the Lord your God has commanded you; do not turn aside to the right or to the left. Walk in all the way that the Lord your God has commanded you, so that you may LIVE and prosper and prolong your days in the land that you will posses.

I pray that all things may go well as we ask God for strength and guidance each day. Let us be watchful of keeping His commands and putting Him first in our lives. The rewards are great.

Have a prosperous day!

Day 64
A WISE WOMAN BUILDS HER HOUSE

What a great responsibility God has given woman to build her house. He knows that we are capable to do the job well. We either bring it to life or to destruction. Use every effort, mentally, physically, and spiritually to build up your home. God created woman in such a unique way; He knew only a woman could fulfill and support a man. That is why He created Eve for Adam. We are also nurturers by heart, and multi-taskers. That is how we can keep the family unit intact. Pray that God will help direct your power in a good and edifying way.

It is very important to learn to communicate in a healthy manner. Our body language, tone of voice and choice of words speak volumes. As we stay plugged into God each day, yield to the strength and power of the Holy Spirit and receive confidence in Christ. Let us help build our husband and children's confidence. I pray that the Spirit will speak to your heart and direct you in the right way to build up your home. It is never too late to start.

Proverbs 14:1 Every wise woman builds her house but the foolish one tears it down with her own hands.

Let us step forward and move towards the right direction in building up, up, and continuously up!

Have an edifying day!

Day 65
A FIGHT WORTH FIGHTING FOR

We all have set certain goals in our lives at one time or another. How about setting a goal for ourselves to be the best person we can be for God's glory? Let us have purpose, meaning, and be useful for God's kingdom with all that God has shaped us to be.

Pastor Rick Warren describes the meaning of the word, S.H.A.P.E: **S**piritual Gifts, Unique **H**eart, Our **A**bilities, **P**ersonality, Our Life's **E**xperiences. If we use our," SHAPE" for God's Kingdom and reach our goals to win the prize, (the crown of righteousness), handed over to us from Almighty God Himself, tears of joy will overflow!

2 Timothy 4:7-8 I have fought the good fight, I have finished the race, I have kept the faith. Now there is in store for me the crown of righteousness, which the Lord, the righteous Judge, will award to me on that day - and not only to me, but also to all who have longed for his appearing.

Now, that's a fight worth fighting for! Let us be encouraged to continue to firmly hold on to our precious faith and finish our race to win. If we fall, do not quit. Pick yourself back up and keep on running the race set before you. Your ultimate prize will be worth the fight!

Have a motivated day!

Day 66
PRISONER OF HOPE

How can we activate words such as *astonishment, marvel, bewilderment* and *beyond awesome* in our own lives? Only when we feel like we are at a bottomless pit in our lives and it seems that there is no way out. As we grasp onto hope and become prisoners to it, we have no choice but to keep on hoping in dreary, hopeless situations.

Zechariah 9:12   Return to the stronghold (of security and prosperity), you prisoners of hope; even today do I declare that I will restore double your former prosperity to you.

As prisoners, we are held captive. Let us be continuously captivated by the promises of God's hope in our lives.

Psalm 39:2   He drew me up out of a horrible pit, out of the miry clay (froth and slime) and set my feet upon a rock, steadying my steps and establishing my goings.

Only through God and all His being, our feet are set upon a rock which brings us stability. He will help lift us up from any despair, but we must also do our part and have the willingness to rise up. Pray for patience and wisdom and be thankful that we are prisoners of hope. Everything good about God is hope. Keep it alive and activated.

Have a very hopeful day!

YOU ARE THE HOME OF THE HOLY SPIRIT

When we guard something, we actively protect it because it has great value to us. God wants us to guard and protect the truth of His words in our hearts by the help of His Spirit. Do not allow or let His precious words slip away, and do not ignore them. Put them inside the safe box of your heart and lock them up with the key of His Sprit.

2 Timothy 1:14 Guard and keep (with the greatest care) the precious and excellently adapted (Truth) which has been entrusted (to you), by the (help of the) Holy Spirit Who makes His home in us.

As believers in Christ, the Spirit lives inside of us and we are His dwelling place. He helps us to always remember God's precious words and to meditate on them bringing them to life to give us peace, hope and joy. We are so privileged to have God's Holy Spirit live inside of us. His Spirit comforts, leads and guides us. It speaks to us; strengthens and empowers us; and is always with us. How much better can that be than for us to be His dwelling place? We are His home. Let us make the Spirit comfortable living inside of us as we go on our journey of life together. Make Him your best friend.

Have a secured day!

Day 68
WHO TAKES THE CREDIT?

Pride in our own ability is an enemy! When we elevate ourselves too much and take all credit of our skills, talents and abilities, then don't be alarmed if one day they are taken away from you. Pride can make us judgmental and full of ourselves. The enemy loves that and wants us to be blinded by all truths.

1 Corinthians 4:7 For who separates you from the others? (Who makes you superior and sets you apart from another, giving you the preeminence?) What have you that was not given to you? If then you received it (from someone), Why do you boast as if you had not received (but had gained it by your own efforts)?

God alone gives all of the talents, abilities, and gifts that we need to succeed in life. He equips us to excel! He is the true source and giver.

Job 10:8 Your hands shaped me and made me.

Instead of boasting in and of ourselves, we should boast and give all glory and thankfulness to God!

Isaiah 43:21 The people I have shaped for myself will broadcast my praises.

Let's be aware and remind ourselves that everything we are and everything we have comes as a wonderful gift from God. God is so good!

Have a humbling day!

Day 69
IT CAN ALL COME AND GO

It is very important that we take notice of all the good things in our lives, such as wonderful relationships, blessed possessions, and positions here on earth. We work hard for these things, which are favor and blessings, so we must embrace them all. Nothing in life is permanent so we need to have a content attitude and a heart of gratefulness, for one day it is here, and one day it can be gone.

1 Timothy 6:7 After all, we didn't bring anything with us when we came into the world and we certainly cannot carry anything with us when we die.

So let us truly embrace all that we have and not strive to chase after the wind, trying to accumulate all the "stuff" here on earth.

Job 1:21 Naked I came from my mother's womb, and naked I will depart. The Lord gave and the Lord has taken away; may the name of the Lord be praised.

God Himself wants to be bigger than all the things on earth that we have! Our relationship with Him is everlasting and eternal! As we live, let us not have the mentality of "whoever has more toys wins," but instead have the attitude that *God is our everything*! God wants us to love Him with all our mind, heart and soul. Let us be reminded to seek a right perspective daily and learn to be content and honor God in everything.

Have a pondering day!

PLEASE GOD, NOT MEN

Do you find yourself at a hard place when you have to take orders from someone who is at a higher position than you? In the presence of terrible bosses, our flesh just naturally loves to retaliate!

Colossians 3:23-24 Whatever may be your task, work at it heartily (from the soul), as (something done) for the Lord and not for men. Knowing that it is from the Lord (and not from men) that you will receive the inheritance which is your (real) reward. (The one whom you are actually serving is) the Lord Christ.

God looks at your heart's attitude in your response to orders from our earthly masters. He wants us to obey them from our motivation of our own reverence and fear of the Lord; because we want to please Him in all that we do. Be sincere and work hard at what you do with all your heart and soul. Then, your rewards from God will overflow with His wonderful blessings. That's what truly counts. Let's make God proud.

Have a rightfully focused day!

Day 71
BEING IN PREPARATION

When you want to make a great meal and already know what is on the menu, you start out by preparing for it. You go out and buy the ingredients, chop up the vegetables, organize the bowls and utensils to be used, etc.. God already knows the plans He has for you in order to do His good works!

Ephesians 2:10 For we are God's workmanship, created in Christ Jesus to do good works, which God prepared in advance for us to do.

As we live out our lives, God is there to prepare us and use us for His glory. When we go through the good times as well as the difficult, trying times, He is right there with you actively working in you and preparing your heart and skills for His ultimate good. Meanwhile, trust in Him and know that He has a good plan for you in your life.

Philippians 1:6: ...being confident of this, that He who began a good work in you will carry it on to completion until the day of Christ Jesus.

Let us not resist to God's plan, instead be open and willing to cooperate with Him, having our thoughts in line with His will. What a great privilege and honor it is to be used by God!

Have an obliging day!

Day 72
ALWAYS AND CONSISTENTLY HAVE THE SHOW-OFF-ATTITUDE

Are you the type of person who likes to show off to the people you want to impress? It could be your boss at work, your teacher, or that special someone in your life. But God wants us to do our very best consistently, especially when *no one is around*!

Philippians 2:12-14 Therefore, my dear ones, as you have always obeyed, so now not only (with the enthusiasm you would show) in my presence but much more because I am absent, work out your own salvation with reverence and awe and trembling (self-distrust, with serious caution, tenderness of conscience, watchfulness against temptation, timidly shrinking from whatever might offend God and discredit the name of Christ). (Not in your own strength) for it is God Who is all the while effectually at work in you (energizing and creating in you the power and desire), both to will and to work for His good pleasure and satisfaction and delight.

Let us fight against laziness; instead, let us press on toward our goal to live an energized life through faith with God's strength. Especially when no one around is looking! God sees all and that's what truly matters. Let us be encouraged to always and consistently have a *show-off-attitude* in the right way!

Have an impressing day!

Day 73
WE ARE NOT GRASSHOPPERS AMONG THE GIANTS

Have you ever felt overwhelmed by any giant-sized problems in your life? How you look at yourselves and your circumstances during those times of challenges is extremely important.

Numbers 13:33 There we saw the Nephilim (or giants), the sons of Anak, who come from the giants; and we were in our own sight as grasshoppers, and so we were in their sight.

We must remember who and whose we are. We are children of God. Do not be intimidated by the size of your problems. Having the right perspective of who you are projects just that to others. We are strong, capable, confident and more than conquerors through Christ.

Philippians 4:13 I have strength for all things in Christ Who empowers me.

If we choose to see ourselves as cowardly grasshoppers, the results will be misery, pain, defeat and destruction. God strategically places us in positions to win our battles.

1 Samuel 17:47 for the battle is the Lord's, and He will give you into our hands.

With the power of God's might, you can win any battles because God is always with you. Let us be confident, patient, and trusting in God. Let us always stay in faith. Victory is the Lord's!

Have a courageous day!

Day 74
BEING PRECIOUS IN GOD'S SIGHT

Is anyone interested in being precious in God's sight? The saying goes, "Beauty is in the eye of the beholder." God looks on the inward beauty of a pure heart and all its attributes.

1 Peter 3:4 But let it be the inward adoring and beauty of the hidden person of the heart, with the incorruptible and unfading charm of a gentle and peaceful spirit, which is very precious in the sight of God.

Let us have and maintain a pure heart by our thoughts, motives, attitudes, and actions. The quietness of a gentle soul and peace within is very attractive to God. By developing good habits, little by little, we eventually take out the junk and purify our hearts. God is patient, as He works with us through the Holy Spirit to help, to cleanse, and to purify us.

Proverbs 4:23 Keep and guard your heart with all vigilance and above all that you guard, for out of it flow the springs of life.

Let's be encouraged to work on our hearts and choose to have inner purity which honors and glorifies God.

Have a refining day!

Day 75
AN APPOINTED TIME

God's time table is not like ours. One year to us can be one day to Him. As God sets an appointed time to answer our prayers, let us receive blessings, and do great things. He wants us to eagerly wait on Him with great anticipation.

Habakkuk 2:3   For the vision is yet for an appointed time and it hastens to the end (fulfillment); it will not deceive or disappoint. Though it tarry, wait (earnestly) for it, because it will surely come; it will not be behindhand on its appointed day.

During the time of waiting, we undergo immense character growth. Maybe sometimes He purposely does not answer our prayers because He wants us to grow in Him by testing our faith, patience, endurance and trust. We must wait with a good attitude and not allow our impatience to take over. Through acts of impatience and resistance, we may attempt steps toward our own plans but delay receiving God's blessings.

Genesis 18:14   Is anything too hard or too wonderful for the Lord? At the appointed time, when the season (for her delivery) comes around, I will return to you and Sarah shall have borne a son.

Thank God that there is nothing too hard for Him. God rewards your faithfulness and obedience.

Have a hopeful and expectant day!

Day 76
THERE IS NO OTHER GIFT THAT COMPARES

Have you ever yearned for or desired a particular gift, never to receive it? Or perhaps, you always seem to get what you want. There is a priceless gift given to us by our Almighty God, His son, Jesus Christ. We are valued by God and because of God's abundant love and kindness for us, He gave us His son, who lived on earth and died for our sins. What a wonderful sacrifice. There is no other gift that can compare to that. The gift of Jesus completely fills you up, because God is love. Only God knew to what extent we needed to be saved from our own sins and gave us the miraculous gift of Jesus's birth to save us from our sinful selves. Praise God for His glorious, magnificent gift.

Matthew 1:21 She will give birth to a son, and you are to give him the name Jesus, because he will save his people from their sins.

It can't get any more significant than that. Let us always take the time to remember the true reason for the Christmas season. We thank you and praise you, Lord!

Have a magnificent day!

BE ASSURED AND PROCLAIM YOUR VICTORY

How do you view the challenges and difficulties that you face in life? Let's be assured and proclaim our victory! Don't shrink back from them with trembling and fear. Rather, be bold and courageous knowing with Christ you can conquer anything! As believers, the power of Christ is in you.

1 Corinthians 15:57-58 But thanks be to God, Who gives us the victory (making us conquerors) through our Lord Jesus Christ. Therefore, my beloved brethren, be firm (steadfast), immovable, always abounding in the work of the Lord (always being superior, excelling, doing more than enough in the service of the Lord), knowing and being continually aware that your labor in the Lord is not futile (it is never wasted or to no purpose).

God can use your hardships as a stepping stone to raise you to a new level of faith! Be firm and do the very best you can, being consistently aware that all the good and right things you do is never wasted in God's kingdom. God never wastes any challenges you go through, but He always uses them for the greater good in your life. Keep on trusting in Him no matter what and have faith in the divine plan that He has made out for you.

Have a proclaiming day!

Day 78
BELIEVE POSITIVELY

Is there a way to believe positively? Some of us may believe negatively with doubts, laziness and discouragements constantly nagging at us. God wants us to Have faith in Him, and believe without a doubt that He will fulfill His promises to us. Abraham held on to God's promise of giving Him a son, even when it took years for that to happen. In the meantime, he was steadfast in his faith and his confidence grew as his faith grew stronger, always praising and glorifying God!

Romans 4:18-21 Yet he did not waver through unbelief regarding the promise of God, but was strengthened in his faith and gave glory to God, being fully persuaded that God had power to do what He had promised. This is why it was credited to him as righteousness.

What a great example for us as believers to follow. We need to seek, lean and trust in God and in all His ways. He has the power to do the impossible!

Hebrews 11:6 And without faith it is impossible to please God, because anyone who comes to Him must believe that He exists and that He rewards those who earnestly seek Him.

Let us build up excitement as we look forward to what God has planned for our lives! Believing positively brings much hope, excitement, and joy to our lives. Let us Praise God and keep on Praising God no matter what!

Have a faith-filled day!

Day 79
A SPECTACULAR REASON TO REJOICE

We can deceive ourselves by thinking that we can get filled up by all the possessions, prestige, and power we may have. The truth is that we are made full in Christ alone.

Colossians 2:10 and you have been given fullness in Christ, who is the head over every power and authority.

In His fullness, we receive healing in every way, peace and are made whole and new.

Isaiah 53:5 But He was pierced for our transgressions, he was crushed for our iniquities; the punishment that brought us peace was upon Him, and by his wounds we are healed.

Wow! Jesus already suffered and paid the price for us to be alive and whole in Him! He knew He had to go through the sufferings in order to save us. By His choice of obedience to God's plan, purpose and will for Him, we are saved. Now, that's a spectacular reason to rejoice. I pray God's Spirit will speak to your heart today!

Have a beautiful and joyous day!

Day 80
HOW COULD I GO ON?

Have you noticed in times of our flesh, we think we have no strength to go on during trials in life or have no ability to do certain tasks? But, somehow we are able to go on and accomplish what needs to be done, wondering to ourselves, how in the world and where did my strength come from?

2 Timothy 2:1 So you, my son, be strong (strengthened inwardly) in the grace (spiritual blessing) that is (to be found only) in Christ Jesus.

God is our source of strength and with His power, His grace, and His favor are we able to keep on keeping on in the tough times. Let us think back at the challenging times in our life and praise God that He was able to help carry us through. He promises to be with us and help us in our past, present and future! Hold on to His wonderful promises and find your divine strength from only Christ. Pray every day for God's strength, grace and spiritual blessings. It all starts from the inside. Abide in Him!

Have the most assured day!

Day 81
FROM THE OLD, TO THE BRAND NEW YOU

Sometimes we may think, act, and say things that we don't realize are wrong. Or maybe we do know, but just can't help or control it. It may feel like something has possessed us. There is a way to change from the old you, to the brand new you in Christ!

Ephesians 2:3-5 All of us also lived among them at one time, gratifying the cravings of our sinful nature and following its desires and thoughts. Like the rest we were by nature objects of wrath. But because of His great love for us, God, who is rich in mercy, made us alive with Christ even when we were dead in transgressions- it is by grace you have been saved.

Ephesians 2:8 For it is by free grace (God's unmerited favor) that you are saved (delivered from judgment and made partakers of Christ's salvation) through (your) faith. And this (salvation) is not of yourselves (of your own doing, it came not through your own striving), but it is the gift of God.

The most wonderful gift of God's free salvation is offered and given to us. Let us take Him up on it and live in the blessed abundant life in Christ. Thank you Lord for Your love and kindness toward us.

Have a liberating day!

Day 82
YOUR ATTITUDE MATTERS

How do you look at your troubles? Do you shrink in fear, do you think of the worst possible scenario, and do you dread its forthcoming? Perhaps another option is remembering our Almighty God and trusting in His sovereignty, obeying Him in everything with a good attitude.

2 Corinthians 2:9 For this was my purpose in writing you, to test your attitude and see if you would stand the test, whether you are obedient and altogether agreeable (to following my orders) in everything.

Sounds pretty tough? Only we have the power to choose our attitude. No one can force us in that department! I pray that we will choose what is good, right and agreeable to God's will in our life. All wonderful things start with a good attitude. Don't you agree? Let's be encouraged to try it and see what happens. If you want to instantly feel better, than change your attitude towards the good.

Have a happy and mighty day!

Day 83
GO FOR GOD'S DIRECTION

Notice how we often ask ourselves, what should I do? We can try to come up with several different answers and still be confused! God wants us to go for God's direction.

Proverbs 3:5-6 Trust in the Lord with all your heart and lean not on your own understanding; in all your ways acknowledge Him, and He will make your path straight.

Let's be honest, it can be of great challenge to trust in God with certain things, but that is all He ask of us! If we acknowledge Him in our decision making, He *will* guide us! When we choose to do that, tremendous blessings comes our way.

Isaiah 58:11 And the Lord shall guide you continually and satisfy you in drought and in dry places and make strong your bones. And you shall be like a watered garden and like a spring of water whose waters fail not.

Doesn't that sound good to you? What a wonderful place to be at, and great rewards await us as we continue to trust in God with our daily decisions. Let us get rid of our independent ways of thinking and instead trust in God's blueprint for our lives!

Have a most fulfilled day!

Day 84
LOVING THE UNLOVELY?

What comes to mind when you think of the word, *love*? Naturally we tend to love people close and dear to our hearts, but what about loving the unlovely, difficult ones? That is quite a challenge, especially when they offend you or deliberately hurt you.

1 John 4:7-8 Dear friends, let us love one another, for love comes from God. Everyone who loves has been born of God and knows God. Whoever does not love does not know God, because God is love.

Everything about God is love, so let us abide in Him and choose to love others. Jesus gave us a perfect example to follow. When the people ridiculed Him, beat and crucified Him, He prayed to God.

Luke 23:34 Jesus said, "Father, forgive them, for they do not know what they are doing."

We are all broken people, but only in Christ is love alive and forgiveness found. Let us pray that God will help to soften our hearts today and follow in Jesus' great example of love and forgiveness. God will be pleased and peace will enter your hearts.

Have a forgiving day!

DESIRE PERFECT PEACE?

What can we do when we are anxious and worried? Turn your thoughts to God so that you can experience His perfect peace.

Isaiah 26:3-4 You will guard him and keep him in perfect and constant peace whose mind (both its inclination and its character) is stayed on your, because he commits himself to you, leans on you, and hopes confidently in you. So trust in the Lord (commit yourself to Him, lean on Him, hope confidently in Him) forever; for the Lord God is an everlasting rock (the Rock of Ages).

It can't get any better than that! Let's keep our mind stayed on God for that perfect peace.

Proverbs 3:5-6 Lean on, trust in, and be confident in the Lord with all your heart and mind and do not rely on your own insight or understanding. In all your ways know, recognize, and acknowledge Him, and He will direct and make straight and plain your paths.

What a relief to know that God is here to guide, direct and give us perfect peace.

Have a settled day!

Day 86
WHAT A DIFFERENCE YOU CAN MAKE

We may think that just one person cannot make a difference, but how wrong that perspective can be. You can make that much of a difference when you choose to obey God in your own life having the affect on other's all around you, such as your spouse, children, friends, co-workers and community.

Romans 5:19 For just as by one man's disobedience (failing to hear, heedlessness, and carelessness) the many were constituted sinners, so by one man's obedience the many will be constituted righteous (made acceptable to God, brought into right standing with Him).

By your obedience and right actions, you can help others to be brought to righteousness for generations to come. You can be the one person who makes a tremendous, significant difference in some one's life! You have that power and ability whether you realize it or not. Our enemy knows that all too well, so, let us not give into his lies and deceit by being disobedient towards God. Rather, choose and walk in righteousness and receive the abundant, overflowing blessings that come along with it.

Have a day that makes a difference!

Day 87
TAP INTO YOUR OWN UNIQUENESS

Let us learn to accept ourselves and how God made and designed us and let us tap into our own gifts and talents given to us by God, so as to use them for His plan.

1 Corinthians 12:27 Now you (collectively) are Christ's body and (individually) you are members of it, each part severally and distinct (each with his own place and function).

Do not compete and compare with others. If we try to always keep up with others and try to become like them, we are left only with frustrations and less joy. Know and accept who you are in Christ and tap into your own uniqueness and your own spiritual gifts and make them useful for God's kingdom. Let us thank God always and trust in Him for everything. One of the keys to enjoying your life and not missing out on the beautiful life God has planned especially for you is to be satisfied and happy with yourself and with where you're at. God's goodness is all around you. Let's be encouraged to open up our spiritual eyes and see.

Have an embracing day!

Day 88
AMAZING GRACE, HOW SWEET THE SOUND

As believers, by accepting Jesus death on the cross, we automatically receive a life under the umbrella of God's surpassing favor and grace!

Ephesians 2:7 He did this that He might clearly demonstrate through the ages to come the immeasurable (limitless, surpassing) riches of His free grace (His unmerited favor) in (His) kindness and goodness of heart toward us in Christ Jesus.

It was by Jesus death and resurrection that all our sins were paid for. We no longer have to live by the law anymore, feeling condemned or guilty for our sins! God's kindness and goodness to us as His children far surpasses any rules and regulations in our lives by the umbrella of His grace. His grace is given freely to us! How great and awesome is our God and His wonderful love! His amazing grace saves us from ourselves and our wretc.hedness.

God's grace enlightens us to see God in and through everything in our lives. It just sounds too good to be true that God's grace is a free gift to us all! All we have to do is accept His grace and know that we live under his favor and blessings, whether we make mistakes or not! Being hard on ourselves is a waste of time. Let us recognize God and give Him all praise and glory that He so deserves.

Have a marvelous day!

Day 89
ANGELS OF PROTECTION

Have you ever been in a near death situation and sensed the angels of God protecting you? Or maybe, you were stuck in a bad place in your life and God used certain people (seemingly angels) to speak truth to you and helped guide and direct you in the right direction. Either way, God uses His angels to protect us from evil, harm and danger.

Psalm 91:9-11   If you make the Most High your dwelling -- even the Lord, who is my refuge -- then no harm will befall you, no disaster will come near your tent. For he will command his angels concerning you to guard you in all your ways.

As believers, what a great comfort knowing that God's angels are at work in our lives. There is a plan and purpose in your life for God's will to be done. The angels are here to help us and to see it through by accompanying, defending, and preserving us in all our ways. You have your very own guardian angel! Thank you God for your Angels of Protection.

Have a comforting day!

Day 90
READY FOR A NEW THING?

Is there something in your past that is holding you back? Does it just seem very difficult to forget and let go? How can we move forward when we are holding onto the things of old?

Isaiah 43:18 Forget the former things, do not dwell on the past. See, I am doing a new thing! Now it springs up; do you not perceive it? I am making a way in the desert and streams in the wasteland.

God is waiting for you to let go of the pain of past issues: hardships, grudges, jealousies, conflicts, etc.. All the while, He is at work preparing a path of new ventures for you by making a way out of your desert and putting beauty in your life. Sound good? Let us accept and take up God's offer of doing a new thing in our lives.

Have a bold day!

Day 91
DEALING WITH OTHERS

Why does it have to be so hard and challenging when dealing with others? Dr. Wayne Dyer says, "Never overestimate the power to change others; Never underestimate the power to change yourself." There is great truth to that statement! It can be so frustrating when we try to make someone else the way *we* want them to be, never realizing that we have the most power to change *ourselves*!

Luke 6:37   Judge not, and you will not be judged; forgive and release (give up resentment, let it drop) and you will be forgiven and released.

We release true joy into our lives by not judging, by forgiving and by giving up resentments that has been building up for some time.

Psalm 51:10-12 Create in me a pure heart, O God, and renew a right, persevering, and steadfast spirit within me. Cast me not away from Your presence and take not Your Holy Spirit from me. Restore to me the joy of Your salvation and uphold me with a willing spirit.

Pray that God will work on our hearts today as we desire peace and joy in all our valued relationships. Let us be sensitive to the Holy Spirit to help lead and guide the way.

Have an understanding day!

Day 92
SEE YOURSELF AS A GOOD THREAT

As believers, whenever we grow in our faith and do what's good for God's kingdom, we hold the power of threatening the enemy. He does not like it one bit and he will try to take you down by distractions that will pull you away from God.

1 Peter 5:8 Be self controlled and alert. Your enemy ... prowls around like a roaring lion looking for someone to devour.

Do not allow that to happen! Whenever you face struggles of any kind, look to it as a manner in which you are doing something good for God and being a threat to negativity. Rise above your struggles and keep focusing your faith and trust in God no matter what! Have patience as God works behind the scenes to help pull you out of the hardships. God is always in the process of refining you for a greater use for His kingdom.

Hebrews 12:10-11 Our fathers disciplined us for a little while as they thought best; but God disciplines us for our good, that we may share in His holiness. No discipline seems pleasant at the time, but painful. Later on, however, it produces a harvest of righteousness and peace for those who have been trained by it.

Let us be encouraged when faced with trials, to see yourself as a good threat to the enemy being trained for our harvest of righteousness and peace!

Have a positive, training day!

TAKE THE FIRST STEP

Is there something that you've always wanted to do, but for whatever reason, you never had the time or courage to do it? We are always making excuses, but there really is no excuse.

Isaiah 60:1 Arise, shine, for your light has come and the glory of the Lord rises upon you.

With faith, having God's strength and His might within you, all things are possible! The things tugging at your heart that is God-ordained, such as goals, projects, endeavors, and adventures, can be accomplished. If we just sit around and do nothing, then nothing gets done and we miss out on all of life's goodness that God has in store for us. Let's be encouraged to arise and take the first step and be bold and courageous to try new things with God's blessings and favor on our side. You will truly be astonished and give God praise.

Have a stirred up day!

Day 94
THE HEART AND MOUTH CONNECTION

If you haven't checked in lately to how your *heart* connection is doing, then, pay attention to the words that come out of your *mouth*. Are they positive, edifying words, or negative, destroying words? There is a very strong connection to the heart and the mouth!

Matthew12:34-36 You brood of vipers, how can you who are evil say anything good? For out of the overflow of the heart the mouth speaks. The good man brings good things out of the good stored up in him, and the evil man brings evil things out of the evil stored up in him. But I tell you that men will have to give account on the Day of Judgment for every careless word they have spoken.

If we practice the art of listening to others, we can tell what kind of a person they are by the fruits they produce in their lives and their speech. Let us be known by our good fruits by saying good words. Whatever you think, it's going to come out of your mouth.

James 3:10 Out of the same mouth come praise and cursing. My brothers, this should not be.

Let us pray for the Spirit of self control to help us daily to control our thoughts and words and make them only pleasing to God.

Have a disciplined day!

Day 95
DON'T BE SURPRISED AT YOUR SUFFERINGS

When we go through the painful trials in our lives, we may think to ourselves, "I can't believe this is happening to me!" As believers, God tells us not to be surprised or alarmed at our struggles, but to keep on rejoicing. What, are you serious?

1 Peter 4:12-13 Dear friends, do not be surprised at the painful trial you are suffering, as though something strange were happening to you. But rejoice that you participate in the sufferings of Christ, so that you may be overjoyed when His glory is revealed.

Through our sufferings, we get closer to God and it keeps us humble. At the end, we know that we will receive an award, the crown of Life that God has set aside and promised to us.

1 Peter 4:19 So then, those who suffer according to God's will should commit themselves to their faithful Creator and continue to do good.

The key while in the process of sufferings, is to keep on doing good! Let us be encouraged to endure and to keep our eyes fixed and committed to God, trusting in His sovereignty. He has a good plan for you.

Have a rejoicing day!

Day 96
YOU WILL SOAR

Have you ever felt that you were incapable of doing great things? You know you have the ability to do little things, but that's about it? Think again! With God on your side and He being a master in your field, together, you can soar. You will be able to do magnificent things, beyond what you've imagined.

Ephesians 3:20 Now to Him who is able to do immeasurably more than all we ask or imagine, according to His power that is at work within us, to Him be glory in the church and in Christ Jesus throughout all generations, forever and ever!

There's a story of a little boy who plays the song *Chopsticks* on the piano on-stage before a concert. Later, the master pianist tells him not to stop and joins him, together playing a magnificent masterpiece. Let's be encouraged to keep endeavoring and never quit whatever your music in life may be. Together with God on your side, you can and will soar.

Have a magnificent day!

Day 97
BUT IT'S TOUGH

Have you ever experienced overwhelming stress and uncontrollable emotions when going through hardships? You thought the day would never end and that you would always feel like that!

Psalm 30:5 Weeping may endure for a night, but joy comes in the morning.

Thank goodness we have hope for a new day.

Hebrews 13:5 God, Himself has said, I will not in any way fail you nor give you up nor leave you without support. (I will) not, (I will) not, (I will) not in any degree leave you helpless nor forsake nor let (you) down (relax My hold on you!

Somehow after sleeping, our next-day emotions are not as intense and hope for a new day sets within.

Psalm 126:5 They who sow in tears shall reap in joy and singing.

Always remember that God is with you during the tough times. He'll never, ever leave you nor forsake you. Hold on to His promise that this, too, shall pass.

Have a comforting day!

Day 98
PURIFY INTO PERFECTING HOLINESS

As we grow into our spiritual maturity, there are requests given unto us from God for our benefit.

2 Corinthians 7:1 Since we have these promises, dear friends, let us purify ourselves from everything that contaminates body and spirit, perfecting holiness out of reverence for God.

Let us honor God in all that we do!

James 1:21 Therefore, get rid of all moral filth and the evil that is so prevalent and humbly accept the word planted in you, which can save you.

Let us yield and allow the work of the Holy Spirit to work on our soul for our salvation. The soul is often defined as the mind, the will, and the emotions. Let us not reject God's teachings, but rather embrace and love His words and have them deeply planted and secured in our hearts. God graciously and lovingly gives us His words to save our soul in every way. Let us apply them into our lives, and be encouraged to humbly aim to grow into maturity of holiness out of our reverential fear and awe of God.

Have a purifying day!

Day 99
BEING IN THE PROCESS OF GOD'S PLAN

Did you know that God has a good plan for us? His plan is for us to do good works!

Ephesians 2:10   For we are God's workmanship, created in Christ Jesus to do good works, which God prepared in advance for us to do.

Imagine that! Kay Marshall Strom has said, "Our job and experiences are preparing us for our second half in life. Use those skills that are prepared for, now; use them for significance in the latter half of your life." All that we go through in our lives are preparing us to do good works for God's glory! We are in the process of God's plan whether we know it or not, and his plan for us is grander than our own plans. If we are dealing with struggles or have made mistakes, get back in line with agreement to His plan and purpose, by trusting and obeying Him.

Jeremiah 29:11   For I know the plans I have for you, declares the Lord, plans to prosper you and not to harm you, plans to give you hope and a future.

God's good plan is where you want to be, full of life, health, happiness, and fulfillment in every way.

Have a productive day!

Day 100
LET US REMEMBER AND GIVE THANKS

Let us remember that the small things, as well as the big things, God has done for you. You wouldn't be who and where you are today if it wasn't for His love and faithfulness towards you.

Psalm 105:5   (Earnestly) remember the marvelous deeds that He has done, His miracles and wonders.

Let's make it a habit to recall God's faithfulness in our lives and always thank Him. Let us continue to build our faith in Him and trust that He will always take care of us no matter what.

1 Thessalonians 5:18   Thank (God) in everything (no matter what the circumstances may be, be thankful and give thanks), for this is the will of God for you (who are) in Christ Jesus (the Revealer and Mediator of that will).

Take the time to think of all your past blessings and thank God for them. God is so good.

Have a grateful day!

Day 101
YOU HAVE WHAT IT TAKES

Sometimes, we think that we don't have what it takes to be "good." We call ourselves short on many things. God tells us the importance of daily renewing our minds and putting on, with effort, our new nature of goodness and righteousness in Him.

Ephesians 4:23-24 And be constantly renewed in the spirit of your mind (having a fresh mental and spiritual attitude). And put on the new nature (the regenerate self) created in God's image, (Godlike) in true righteousness and holiness.

See, you have what it takes. All you have to do is constantly renew your way of thinking with the right biblical attitude and put the effort on becoming more Christ-like. He sets a wonderful example in the bible on what to think and how to live from His word. If you truly desire to change for the good, then pray for God's Spirit to strengthen, help, and guide you each and every day. You do have what it takes. Make it a practice and before you know it, you will have a flow of goodness in your life.

Have an enlightening day!

Day 102
BUILDING EACH OTHER UP IN HARMONY

Words cannot describe heart-felt gratitude that one has for another. When we have the love, support, thankfulness, and encouragements from others, it puts a smile on God's face as well as on ours. Something magnificent happens when we look beyond ourselves and reach out to others.

Philippians 2:4 Let each of you esteem and look upon and be concerned for not (merely) his own interests, but also each for the interests of others.

That is what you call true joy.

Romans15:2 Let each one of us make it a practice to please his neighbor for his good and for his true welfare, to edify him (to strengthen him and build him up spiritually).

God tells us to make it a practice and to do it more often. He knows that it builds and encourages ourselves as well.

1 Thessalonians 5:11 Therefore encourage one another and edify (strengthen and build up) one another, just as you are doing.

I encourage you to make it a practice every day to encourage someone, give a hug, be a listening ear, and say encouraging words. You will nourish their souls as well as your own and be blessed. I thank you from the bottom of my heart. God bless!

Have an extraordinary day!

Day 103
THE POWER OF CHOICE

God has given to each and every one of us the power to choose. Every day we make choices, whether big or small. The choices we make have an effect on our circumstances and our futures.

Deuteronomy 30:19 Today I have given you the choice between life and death, between blessings and curses. Now I call on heaven and earth to witness the choice you make. Oh, that you would choose life, so that you and your descendants might live!

Everything good happens to us and those around us when we make the right choices. The results are life and blessings for us and our descendants. We may think that one small bad choice does not matter, but take heed, it does. We reap what we sow, so be aware. Let us think twice when making decisions and choose life. Also, let us not take too lightly our power to choose, but rather embrace it and use it for good. Do not be surprised when abundant blessings come your way. Let us pray that God give us the wisdom and discernment to make good, wise choices.

Have a discerning day!

Day 104
THINGS THAT GOD FORGETS

Is there any sin or deep failure that is holding you back from moving forward? God says and promises that if we confess our sins and ask for forgiveness, He will remember them no more.

1 John 1:9 If we confess our sins, He is faithful and just and will forgive us our sins and purify us from all unrighteousness.

We must confess to God first and ask for forgiveness.

Hebrews 8:12 For I will be merciful and gracious toward their sins and I will remember their deeds of unrighteousness no more.

God says it plain and clear that He will no longer remember your sins.

Psalm 103:12 As far as the east is from the west, so far has He removed our transgressions from us.

We tend to be hard on ourselves at times, but we need to let go of the sins of the past and be freed. As you ask for forgiveness, God says He will forget. Therefore, pray and move on and enjoy the abundant life that lies ahead of you in freedom. The purpose of Jesus's death on the cross is to free us and save us from our sins. Let us remember that God forgives and He forgets! Having faith in Christ is for us to forgive and forget as well. We need to trust Him on that.

Have a liberated day!

Day 105
THE IMPORTANCE TO SHINE

Let us be the light, so that people may wonder what makes us shine so brightly.

Philippians 4:9 Practice what you have learned and received and heard and seen in me, and model your way of living on it. And the God of peace will be with you.

It's a guarantee that God's peace that is always with us makes us shine!

Matthew 5:16 Let your light so shine before men that they may see your moral excellence and your praiseworthy, noble, and good deeds and recognize and honor and praise and glorify your Father Who is in heaven.

God gets all the praise and credit for our brightness and people will come to realize who our God is by our actions and praise Him as well. What a wonderful witness and testimony that is, all by itself! Let us be encouraged to shine, shine, shine some more, so that others can be attracted and warmhearted by our light!

Have a bright day!

Day 106
USE YOUR WEAPON OF THE SWORD

Can you think about something that is powerful, alive, constantly moving, and is the sharpest weapon out there?

Hebrews 4:12 For the word of God is living and active, sharper than any two edged sword.

Let's take a moment and digest this verse. The power of God's word is alive and active within you. It is your daily nourishment for your spiritual soul and a weapon used to attack the enemy. The more we learn the word of God, the stronger its effect on killing any kind of harm, threat, temptation, sin, and ugliness in your life. We should make it a practice to pick up our sword and use the word of God daily against the enemies' attacks. We will always win our battles with God on our side.

Every morning, let us remember to always have our sword with us as a protection and a weapon to fight off the enemy. Victory is ours. Now let us be on guard and attack when necessary. We know the secret of winning our battles.

Have a conquering day!

Day 107
TRUST IN GOD'S MAGNIFICENT TIMING

God's timing is different than what we may want or expect in our lives.

2 Peter 3:8 Nevertheless, do not let this one fact escape you, beloved, that with the Lord one day is as a thousand years and a thousand years as one day. The Lord does not delay and is not tardy or slow about what He promises, according to some people's conception of slowness, but He is long-suffering (extraordinarily patient) toward you, not desiring that any should turn to repentance.

God has His perfect timing in our lives and we must learn to trust Him! He has the appointed season in every matter. We are the ones who are impatient, but with God, there is no difference between one day and a thousand years. Imagine that! When we yield and trust in God's ways, His ways are the best for us. We must give up our independent spirit and allow God to work efficiently and accurately in our lives. The more we resist His timing, the more we delay our hopes and desires. Trust that God will keep His wonderful promises to you! He is very patient with our self-will and stubborn ways. He knows us inside and out and only wants the very best for our lives. When we step back and watch God work intricately and accurately to every detail with His timing, we are marveled with His magnificent ways!

Ecclesiastes 3:11 "He has made everything beautiful in his time.

Have a most patient day!

Day 108
DESIRE JOY?

Anyone interested in being happy and full of joy? Then be a giver by doing good deeds, giving encouraging words, sharing, and being generous with your time, finances, and God given abilities.

1 Timothy 6:18-19 Command them to do good, to be rich in good deeds, and to be generous and willing to share. In this way they will lay up treasure for themselves as a firm foundation for the coming age, so that they may take hold of the life that is truly life.

By following theses commands, you will experience the true life that is intended for you, full of joy and fulfillment in every way. Give it a try especially when you don't feel good. When we step out of ourselves, and put our focus on helping others, the more you give, the more blessings you will receive. It's a guarantee.

Have a heartfelt day!

Day 109
DESIRES OF YOUR HEART

When you have someone who is dear and close to you, with whom you have a wonderful intimate relationship, wouldn't you have the desire to make them happy and to give them desires of their heart?

Psalm 37:4 Delight yourself in the Lord; and He will give you the desires of your heart.

Imagine that! God wants us to be in praise with him intimately, in fellowship and with joy. As He sees us delighting in Him in every way with a genuine heart, He will fill your heart with delight and fulfillment. Only He knows your secret desires and cannot wait to give them to you, in wonder and excitement for what we asked. Be patient and know that it's on its way. Get ready to be marveled! Praise God!

Have an astonishing day!

Day 110
BUILD EACH OTHER UP

How can you contribute to making our world and society a better place? You, yes you, can help and make a difference by the power of your good words.

Romans 15:2 Let each one of us make it a practice to please (make happy) his neighbor for his good and for his true welfare, to edify him (to strengthen him and build him up spiritually).

Let us be in the business of building each other up with encouraging words, rather than tearing one another down. Our words are valuable. Nothing feels better than to have support and encouragement from others. Let's be that person who edifies. When we see a person in need, let us pray to use our words wisely, to help one another and keep building up the body of Christ. Notice when we do our part and choose to use good, positive words that build up, it can rub off on others and have a positive effect.

Have an edifying day!

Day 111
MAKING DECISIONS

When we make choices and decisions in our lives, whether great or small, we are not alone. God is right there to help you through!

Psalm 32:8 I (the Lord) will instruct you and teach you in the way you should go; I will counsel you with my eye upon you.

See, you're never alone! Even those times you think you made the wrong choices, God is right there beside us.

Psalm 37:24 ...though he stumbles, he will not fall, for the Lord upholds him with His hand.

Let us not be so anxious and impatient with our decisions, but take one step at a time knowing that God knows the blueprint for our lives! Trust in Him daily. How far can we go with our finite mind? God's mind is beyond infinite!

Proverbs 3:5-6 Trust in the Lord with all your heart and lean not on your own understanding; in all your ways acknowledge Him, and He will make your paths straight.

Proverbs 16:9 A man's mind plans his way, but the Lord directs His Steps and makes them sure.

The assurance of knowing that you had made the right choice is a sense of peace! Let peace be your guide and assurance! In prayer, always pray for wisdom and discernment through the Holy Spirit.

Have an assured day!

Day 112
SECURED BY THE ARMS OF OUR SHEPHERD

Jesus is our loving good shepherd who knows us all very well and cares for us. If He notices one of His sheep going astray, He will bring us back home with Him.

John 10:14 I am the good shepherd; I know my sheep and my sheep know me -- just as the Father knows me and I know the Father -- and I lay down my life for the sheep.

Jesus is constantly aware and actively guarding and protecting us, making sure that we are secured. He knows our voices as well as we know His, and His greatness and power will be shown to all the earth. Let us follow His voice.

Micah 5-4-5 He will stand and shepherd his flock in the strength of the Lord, in the majesty of the name of the Lord his God. And they will live securely, for then His greatness will reach to the ends of the earth. And he will be their peace.

Peace is the outcome of truly knowing and having a personal, intimate relationship with our Shepherd, Jesus. Trust in Him and be guided by His secured strong and mighty arms.

Have a secured day!

Day 113
DON'T MISS YOUR OPPORTUNITY

Life is full of opportunities! Don't miss you opportunity. If we stop and take notice, there are so many different kinds of opportunities in our path. The opportunity to teach our children well in every good manner, opportunities to say ,"I love you " or "I'm sorry", the opportunity to date a certain person, to take on a new position or change at your work, opportunities to make new friends, the opportunity to search for the things you hope and dream for, and so much more! There are countless opportunities out there.

Philippians 5:15 Be very careful, then, how you live - not as unwise but as wise, making the most of every opportunity, because the days are evil.

Life passes by so quickly and it would be a shame to say to ourselves, "I should have or could have done that!" Let us live our lives purposefully and invest on the good things granted our way. Let us be encouraged to put laziness aside and make good, everlasting memories!

Have a most blessed day!

Day 114
THE CONNECTION BETWEEN OBEDIENCE AND BLESSINGS

Consider some of the things that may get in the way of receiving our blessings. They may be our own self-sufficiency, stubbornness, pride and rebellion.

Deuteronomy 28:2-6 All these blessings will come upon you and accompany you if you obey the Lord your God: You will be blessed in the city and blessed in the country. The fruit of your womb will be blessed, and the crops of your land and the young of your livestock- the calves of your herds and the lambs of your flocks. Your basket and your kneading trough will be blessed. You will be blessed when you come in and blessed when you go out.

Wow, that is a lot of blessings! The longer we hold on to our selfish ways, it will take that much longer to recognize and see our blessings. The connection between obedience and blessings go hand in hand. When we obey God, He is going to take care of us. Let us be encouraged to keep doing what is right and to obey; it's a guarantee that the blessings of the Lord will rain down upon you.

Have an amazed day!

Day 115
OUR LOVING, GOOD SHEPHERD

Let us know more about our good shepherd.

Psalm 23 The Lord is my shepherd, I shall not be in want. He makes me lie down in green pastures, He leads me beside quiet waters, He restores my soul. He guides me in paths of righteousness for His name's sake. Even though I walk through the valley of the shadow of death, I will fear no evil, for you are with me; your rod and your staff, they comfort me. You prepare a table before me in the presence of my enemies. You anoint my head with oil; my cup overflows. Surely goodness and love will follow me all the days of my life, and I will dwell in the house of the Lord forever.

Wow! Do we have an awesome Shepherd or what? He provides for us, He gives us peace and hope, He leads us and tells us not to fear for any reason, because He is always with us to protect, comfort and guide us. He anoints us even before our enemies. Only God's goodness, mercy, and love follow us forever and we shall always be in His presence. Jesus promises to be all that He is to us, our loving, good shepherd.

Have a comforting day!

Day 116
OUR LIFELINE TO SUCCESS IN LIVING

Just imagine yourself, living your life with prosperity, wisdom, and good success. In the world's view, they seem to be achieved by working hard and climbing up the social ladder. In your spiritual life, it is achieved by meditating on the word of God day and night.

Joshua 1:8 This Book of the Law shall not depart out of your mouth, but you shall meditate on it day and night, that you may observe and do according to all that is written in it. For then you shall make your way prosperous, and then you shall deal wisely and have good success.

There are more than plenty issues in life out there that we have to deal with. How do we know which are the right choices to make in good judgment and in wisdom? The key answer is through God's word. When we open the word of God and meditate on what God says, the Spirit helps us in and through many situations in life. As believers, it is our life-line to success in living. Let's be encouraged to fill our minds with God's truth so that we may experience truth, freedom, victory and peace.

Have a rewarding day!

Day 117
CELEBRATE YOUR UNIQUENESS

We can try our best to become like someone else, but we all are different, down to our fingerprints! God intricately and purposefully made us unique and different from one another. How boring it would be if we were all clones and robots. Even twins are different in their personality traits or talents. We should all celebrate our uniqueness!

Psalm 139:15 My frame was not hidden from You when I was being formed in secret (and) intricately and curiously wrought (as if embroidered with various colors) in the depths of the earth (a region of darkness and mystery).

We should tap into our extraordinary talents, gifts and potential that lie from within, and practice using them for God's glory! When we just settle with who and where we are at the moment, it offends God our creator! We are made specially, with much greatness and uniqueness in us!

Verse 13 For you did form my inward parts; You did knit me together in my mother's womb.

See, God knew exactly what He was doing with you even when you were in your mother's womb! As we grow and develop, let us be stretc.hed and challenged to become all that God designed and created us to be. He has a very special plan for your life. Don't compare to others but rather find worth and value in God! Be extraordinary and celebrate your uniqueness. You are one-of-a-kind. Let us be encouraged to be that extraordinary person that God created us to be!

Have a happy day!

Day 118
BE STILL AND KNOW GOD

How can we think clearly, peacefully and make good decisions when there is so much noise and chaos going on? God wants us to be still and to know Him.

Psalm 46:10 Let be and be still, and know (recognize and understand) that I am God. I will be exalted among the nations! I will be exalted in the earth!

In any kind of battles that we deal with, God wants us to hold on to our peace and to be calm, for God will fight our battles for us. Everything is going to be alright!

Exodus 14:14 The Lord will fight for you, and you shall hold your peace and remain at rest.

The key is to be still and to know God and to trust in His almighty strength.

Isaiah 30:15 For thus said the Lord God, the Holy one of Israel: In returning (to Me) and resting (in Me) you shall be saved; in quietness and in (trusting) confidence shall be your strength.

God is your home and refuge; go to Him in the quietness of your faith. Believe that all things will work out for your good.

Have a faith-filled day!

Day 119
HOW'S YOUR ATTITUDE LATELY?

Have you found yourself in a bad attitude lately? Notice when things don't seem to be going your way, it is much easier to settle back in your old habits of thinking and living with complaints and grumblings.

Numbers 14:2-3 All the Israelites grumbled against Moses and Aaron, and the whole assembly said to them, "If only we had died in Egypt! Or in this desert! Why is the Lord bringing us to this land only to let us fall by the sword? Our wives and children will be taken as plunder. Wouldn't it be better for us to go back to Egypt?"

It is important for us to not have the *go-back* mentality. Instead, move forward.

Numbers 21:4-5 They traveled from Mount Hor along the route to the Red Sea, to go around Edom. But the people grew impatient on the way; they spoke against God and against Moses, and said, "Why have you brought us up out of Egypt to die in the desert? There is no bread! There is no water! And we detest this miserable flood!

How easy it is when we are impatient, depressed and discouraged to have a complaining attitude. Hold on to the promise of hope. Let us not give into our negative fleshly ways, but instead keep on persevering. Remember all the good things God has done, and hold on to our promised land of blessings with a good attitude.

Have a hopeful day!

Day 120
SEEK GOD TO REVIVE AND LIVE

Have you wondered to yourself, "Why am I not growing?" Or perhaps, "How come I cannot get out of the turmoil or bondage that I'm in?" God tells us plainly to humble ourselves and to seek Him first! By having fellowship with God as our first priority when we start out our day, it makes all the difference and sets the tone for your day, in His Spirit.

Psalm 42:1 As the deer pants for the water brooks, so pants my soul for You, O God.

As we practice seeking God every day, in time you will have victory!

Psalm 69:32 The humble shall see it and be glad; you who seek God inquiring for and requiring Him (as you first need), let your hearts revive and live!

The greatest benefit we can have in our lives is to be in God's word. It's a guarantee that your life will be revived, as we thrive and live. How marvelous is that?

Have a right focused day!

Day 121
UNSTABLE TIMES

When we go through times of emotional stress and chaos or storms in our lives, let us go to God for stability and security as we lean and rely on Him with all our trust.

Psalm 91:1-4 He who dwells in the secret place of the most High shall remain stable and fixed under the shadow of the Almighty. I will say of the Lord, He is my refuge and my fortress, my God; on Him lean and rely, and in Him I (confidently) trust! For He will deliver you from the snare of the fowler and from the deadly pestilence. (Then) He will cover you with His pinions, and under His wings shall you trust and find refuge; His truth and His faithfulness are a shield and a buckler.

Thank goodness for God's faithfulness to us in providing a place of refuge and safety in Him alone. Let us be encouraged in the midst of unstable times and emotions, to go to God in every way. In and through God are we able to find stability. Let Him be your peace.

Have a stable day!

Day 122
SPIRITUAL TRAINING

Notice when people train for any kind of sports competition or exercise to lose weight, etc., the effort they put into it (the hard work of being diligent, having perseverance, and endurance) eventually pays off, but may not be permanent. But the value of our spiritual training is everlasting!

1 Timothy 4:8   For physical training is of some value, but godliness (spiritual training) is useful and of value in everything and in every way, for it holds promise for the present life and also for the life which is to come.

We are always in the process of our very own spiritual training. The usefulness of it is helpful in everything that we do in our life, at this present time and for the future generations. It is an ongoing training that gets better and better through time. Always stay in faith and know that all the good and bad things that we go through are all part of our spiritual training. It is a gift from God and He has plans and purpose for you and your life.

Have a geared up day!

Day 123
GOD'S PRECIOUS THOUGHTS OF US

Think about someone who is precious in your eyes. They can do no wrong. When you think of that person, good thoughts about them are numerous. That is how our loving Father sees us, as His child.

Psalm 139:17-18 How precious to me are your thoughts, O God! How vast is the sum of them! Were I to count them, they would outnumber the grains of sand. When I awake, I am still with you.

God our creator says, "You're amazing. You're wonderful and you're a masterpiece!"

Psalm 139:13-14 For you created my inmost being; you knit me together in my mother's womb. I praise you because I am fearfully and wonderfully made; your works are wonderful, I know that full well.

God holds us close to His heart and we are always with Him. He thinks the world of us because we are His perfect creation. As we live out our lives, God wants us to please and glorify Him. That is His ultimate plan and purpose for us. As we do just that, let us reverently fear and worship Him in all things.

Have a loving day!

Day 124
WE GET TO WORK

We are privileged people! We have the privileges to go to work, clean our beautiful homes, raise our children, work continually on and enjoy marriages, and so much more! There are many people who would love to be in our position! In our lives, we always have a form of work which we labor under the sun.

Ecclesiastes 5:18-19   Behold, what I have seen to be good and fitting is for one to eat and drink, and to find enjoyment in all the labor in which he labors under the sun all the days which God gives him-for this is his (allotted) part.

We spend a great portion of our time working! What a privilege to have some form of work rather than none! Since we spend a lot of our time working, we have the choice whether to enjoy our work or to dread it, having a bad attitude! Let's be encouraged as we start our work efforts for the day to prematurely thank God for it and have a grateful heart and attitude. That in itself will help us to do our very best, with all excellence enjoying the work God has given graciously to us!

In our lives, there is a time when God gives and a time when He can take away. In the meantime, let us enjoy to the fullest His abundant blessings! When we live our lives in gratitude and in appreciation, then we are able to enjoy our lives even more with true joy.

Have an enjoyable workday!

Day 125
GUARD YOUR MOUTH

Words are powerful. There is a way to prevent your words from getting you into trouble: that is to guard your mouth.

Psalm 141:3 Set a guard, O Lord, before my mouth; keep watch at the door of my lips.

Sometimes, we very much need the help of the Holy Spirit to have the self control to bite our tongues in discernment.

1 Peter 3:9-11 Do not repay evil with evil or insult with insult, but with blessing, because to this you were called so that you may inherit a blessing. For, "Whoever would love life and see good days must keep his tongue from evil and his lips from deceitful speech. He must turn from evil and do good; he must seek peace and pursue it.

If we desire to seek peace, we must do our part and pursue it by living in harmony with one another. Let us have the compassion, humility, love and sympathy to do good.

Psalm 19:14 May the words of my mouth and the meditation of my heart be pleasing in your sight, O Lord, my Rock and my Redeemer.

Let us pray each day for wisdom and guidance to please God with our good choice of words. Then we shall surely see and experience the good days.

Have a discerning day!

Day 126
HONOR GOD IN EVERYTHING

When we think of someone who we honor we put them in the highest respect and admiration, and are in awe of them.

1 Corinthians 10:31 So then, whether you eat or drink, or whatever you may do, do all for the honor and glory of God.

We should be motivated as believers, in everything that we do to honor God. That means the positions given to us as a spouse, parent, worker, friend, etc., makes us strive to be the best God created us to be. Also in doing all our daily tasks, the entertainment that we choose, the words that comes out from out mouth, just about anything you can think of, do it all for the honor and glory of God.

When we have the willingness to do everything for the honor of God, we can do no wrong in His eyes. Then peace, joy, and true contentment will greatly fill your life. By honoring God, it helps you to do what is right, rather than going by how you feel.

Have a glorifying day!

Day 127
**OUR GREAT POWER SOURCE OF
CONNECTION**

What may be our great power source of connection? We are not good for anything if we don't stay connected to our lifeline, which is to abide and remain in Christ.

John 15:5-7 I am the vine; you are the branches. If a man remains in me and I in him, he will bear much fruit; apart from me you can do nothing. If anyone does not remain in me, he is like a branch that is thrown away and withers; such branches are picked up, thrown into the fire and burned. If you remain in me and my words remain in you, ask whatever you wish, and it will be given you.

When we think that we can handle things on our own, don't be surprised when numerous struggles, difficulties and unhappiness come forth. We need our lifeline, which is to stay connected to God. We can do nothing without our source of spiritual nourishment, and being plugged into God will bring fruitfulness in all our endeavors. It fills all our deeds with great significance. In order to have true joy, we must be connected to God!

John 15:11 I have told you this so that my joy may be in you and that your joy may be complete.

Let's keep ourselves connected and plugged into God, activating His Spirit within us at all times.

Have a happy day!

Day 128
YOUR VERY OWN PERSONALIZED PATH

As believers, let us choose to walk the path that God has already planned and prepared for us, to do good works in our lives. Trusting and obeying God are the key foundations to stay on our own path and for us to not go wayward into despair.

Ephesians 2:10 For we are God's (own) handiwork (His workmanship), recreated in Christ Jesus, (born anew) that we may do those good works which God predestined (planned beforehand) for us (taking paths which He prepared ahead of time), that we should walk in them (living the good life which He prearranged and made ready for us to live).

If we truly want and desire to live the good life that God prearranged for us, the sooner we choose to walk that personalized path, the more fulfilling and blessed your life will be. Let us be encouraged to follow in God's good plan for us and to stay on our course made by God and finish our own race well, to win the victorious crown of righteousness. That's a life worth living.

Have a decisive day!

Day 129
NO EXCUSE! GET UP AND WALK!

Ok, enough is enough! Sometimes we can dwell in our own pity party, sufferings, negative thoughts, handicaps etc.. How willing are we to truly want and desire to be well? Don't give into your defeats! There is no excuse!

John 5:6-8 When Jesus saw him lying there and learned that he had been in this condition for a long time, He asked him, "Do you want to get well?" "Sir", the invalid replied, "I have no one to help me into the pool when the water is stirred. While I am trying to get in, someone else goes down ahead of me." Then Jesus said to him, "Get up! Pick up your mat and walk."

Let us not just lie there in our own comfort and weakness, making all the excuses in the book! God commands us to put the effort into being well and to walk. We have to do our part! (verse 9) "At once the man was cured; he picked up his mat and walked." How astounding is that? In all of our struggles, mentally, physically, emotionally, and spiritually, let us believe with all faith, that God will make us well and be free.

Philippians 4:13 I can do everything through Him who gives me strength.

Let us take away the word "excuse" from our mindset and move forward in faith!

Have a victorious day!

Day 130
TAP INTO YOUR AUTHORITY

When we go through challenges and struggles of any kind, it is very important to remember who and to whom you belong. We have been given God's authority in Christ to stand firm and to win our battles.

Luke 10:19 Behold! I have given you authority and power to trample upon serpents and scorpions, and (physical and mental strength and ability) over all the power that the enemy (possesses); and nothing shall in any way harm you.

We must proclaim our God given power and authority. Do not shrink back in fear, but stand with full confidence that you will win your battles just like how little David won the battle against the Giant Goliath. He first proclaimed God's authority to take him on. He had full confidence and poise to defeat the giant. Let's take on that same authority with a confident attitude and power given to us as well. You will surely win.

Have a conquering day!

Day 131
I AM WHAT I AM, BY GOD'S GRACE

Think about how many times your life could have gone in another direction. Or perhaps, you would not have gotten so many chances to be who and where you are today. The grace of God is abundant and living in His grace is where you want to be.

1 Corinthians 15:10 But by the grace (the unmerited favor and blessing) of God I am what I am, and His grace toward me was not (found to be) for nothing (fruitless and without effect). In fact, I worked harder than all of them (the apostles), Though it was not really I, but the grace of God which was with me.

God and His Grace are always with you! No matter what happened or is happening in your life, God is right there to protect, guide, and strengthen you. He pours His wonderful grace upon you. Let us know and recognize all who God is and all the wonderful works that He has done in our lives. Let us continue to be in fellowship with Him, to stay on track in our lives, so we can see and anticipate what more He can make of us through His grace. His grace toward us is fruitful and effective! Praise and thank God for being who you are today by His grace.

Have a pondering day!

Day 132
KNOW YOUR ENEMY WELL TO BE ONE STEP AHEAD OF THE BATTLE

Nobody ever likes to lose. When being chosen to be on a team, we all like to be on the winning side. Well, in the spiritual battle, did you know that Christ and His act of sacrifice on the cross for us already puts us on the winning side to win the battles that we go through in our lives?

1 John 4:4 Little children, you are of God (you belong to Him) and have (already) defeated and overcome them, because He Who lives in you is greater (mightier) than he who is in the world.

People mostly seem to shrink back in fear when they do not know their enemy's schemes or plans of attack. When we become more aware of how our enemy waits for us to let down our guard and attempt to weaken and then attack us, let us look for past triggers and patterns how we had been defeated in those times of negativity's and hardships. His strategies are always the same and common to man. When we become more aware and study the opposing side, we can be a step ahead of them and win victoriously!

1 Peter 5:9 Resist him, standing firm in the faith, because you know that your brothers throughout the world are undergoing the same kind of sufferings.

Let us proclaim we are children of God and stand firm in our faith, being strong, immovable and determined, not to be defeated but to always win our battles against the enemy. Let us look forward to winning with the all powerful God on our side!

Have a victorious day!

Day 133
ENEMIES AT PEACE

God is the only one who has the power and ability to work in people's hearts, even with our enemies.

Proverbs 16:7 When a man's ways please the Lord, He makes even his enemies to be at peace with him.

Consistently doing our part to do what is right and pleasing in God's eyes can even make our enemies be at peace with us. We do not have to be the best of friends, but at least there is peace rather than war. To be able to be near our enemy without hatred, resentment, bitterness, and unforgiveness is worth the true peace that God gives. Stay in faith and live righteously in obedience and there will be peace in due time. God is a pro in doing the impossible. Experiencing God's good works brings awe and joy to our lives.

Have a peaceful day!

Day 134
KILL THE FLESH FOR YOUR BENEFIT

God actually gives us the permission and, in fact, commands us to kill our fleshly appetites.

Colossians 3:5 Put to death, therefore, whatever belongs to your earthly nature: sexual immorality, impurity, lust, evil desires and greed, which is idolatry.

Stop feeding the flesh for every time you feed it, you keep it alive. Let us use the fruit of self control.

Colossians 3:7-10 You used to walk in these ways, in the life you once lived. But now you must rid yourselves of all such things as these: anger, rage, malice, slander, and filthy language from your lips. Do not lie to each other, since you have taken off your old self with its practices and have put on the new self, which is being renewed in knowledge in the image of its creator.

Let us clothe ourselves with the new spiritual self and put ourselves in the process of renewal and remolding into Christ's likeness. The secret is to abide and remain in Christ. Let us pursue righteousness in every area of our lives. Pray that the Holy Spirit will help you and enable you to take action and to kill the flesh for our benefit.

Have a reviving day!

Day 135
BE AWARE AND PAY ATTENTION

It's amazing how our mind can work! It can think about many different things at the same time. It can wander around aimlessly and it can also be trained to stay focused.

Ecclesiastes 5:1 Keep your foot (give your mind to what you are doing) when you go to the house of God. For to draw near and to hear and obey is better than to give the sacrifice of fools (carelessly, irreverently) too ignorant to know that they are doing evil.

God tells us to pay attention, to be aware, and to focus on what we are doing. It is a skill that can be learned over time. We need to stay on track in our walk with God and to keep balance in all that we do. If we allow our minds to wander and do not train our thoughts by discipline, the enemy can make his attack on us. With the combination of his lies and our ignorance, evil is right there to consume us. By meditating on God and all His glory and wondrous works, we train our thoughts to be at peace as we go in the right direction. We do this with God's protection and His good purpose for our lives.

Psalm 145:5 On the glorious splendor of Your majesty and on Your wondrous works I will meditate.

By meditating, it will help you to focus and ponder and to keep your foot on the right track! That is where peace, joy, freedom and victory is to be found.

Have an attentive day!

Day 136
NO NEED TO WORRY

When we are going through difficult, challenging times, fear can arise within us.

Isaiah 41:10 So do not fear, for I am with you; do not be dismayed, for I am your God. I will strengthen you and help you; I will uphold you with my righteous right hand.

God promises that He will be with us and uphold us with His right hand. It can't get any better than that!

Isaiah 43:2 When you pass through the waters, I will be with you, and through the rivers, they will not overwhelm you. When you walk through the fire, you will not be burned or scorched, nor will the flame kindle upon you.

God is your ultimate protection. He will not allow any kind of harm or danger to come upon you.

1 Peter 5:7 Casting the whole of your care (all your anxieties, all your worries, all your concerns, once and for all) on Him, for He cares for you affectionately and cares about you watchfully.

Know in your heart that our faithful, awesome God, who knows the very number of your hair, cares very deeply about you. Let us keep our eyes fixed and focused on Him and trust in His sovereignty!

Have a comforted day!

Day 137
WEIGHED DOWN? BE LIFTED UP!

Why is it so hard to let go of life's difficulties and just cast them upon the Lord to take care of? Do we find ownership in our problems and think to ourselves they are our problems and only we must deal with them? That can weigh you down.

Psalm 55: 22 Cast your cares on the Lord and He will sustain you; he will never let the righteous fall.

God is telling us to give Him our problems, anxieties, struggles and challenges. Trust in Him to take care of them in His ways and timing so that we can be lifted up and sustained to enjoy our lives and relationships peacefully with God.

Isaiah 26:3-4 You will keep in perfect peace him whose mind is steadfast, because he trusts in you. Trust in the Lord forever, for the Lord, the Lord, is the rock eternal.

Let us muster up our faith, believing and trusting that God can and will take care of and handle all our burdens. We just need to cast them in God's direction and He will take hold of them and handle them for you. Release, trust, and be grateful.

Philippians 4:7   And the peace of God, which transcends all understanding, will guard your hearts and your minds in Christ Jesus.

Have a liberating day!

Day 138
ANOTHER MIND IN US?

Most of the time, we automatically assume others think just like we do. How untrue that is! Everyone is different, having their own mindset and ways of thinking. God tells us that we are not alone in our own ways of thinking. We have the mind of Christ! Can you imagine that?

1 Corinthians 2:16 For who has known or understood the mind of the Lord so as to guide and instruct Him and give Him knowledge? But we have the mind of and do hold the thoughts (feelings and purposes) of His heart.

Now that seems inconceivable, doesn't it? How can we think like Jesus?

Ezekiel 36:26-27 And I will put my Spirit within you and cause you to walk in My statutes, and you shall heed My ordinances and do them.

God will give us a new heart and His spirit to live inside of us. He changes us through His holy spirit. In our daily lives, we constantly choose our thoughts or God's thoughts. Let us activate the Spirit within us, being aware and constantly thinking like Christ and His ways, which are good, positive, uplifting, encouraging and a blessing. It's a guarantee of a beautiful, peaceful mind.

Have a right-thinking day!

Day 139
GOD PERFORMS ON YOUR BEHALF

At times, don't we like to think that we can handle our problems and difficulties all on our own? We like to be self-sufficient and we try to tackle hardships by ourselves. But distress, disappointments and helplessness can enter within us. Now what shall we do?

Psalm 57:1-2 Be merciful to me, O God, be merciful to me! For my soul trusts in You; and in the shadow of Your wings I will make my refuge, until these calamities have passed by. I will cry out to God Most High, to God who performs all things for me.

God wants us to worship Him with our whole heart. He wants us to take refuge with peace under the shadow of His wings, with confidence. As we worship and cry out to God, trust and believe that He will hold on to His promises of working on your behalf. He is always working on His purpose in your life, behind the scenes, until it is done! Meanwhile, trust in his sovereignty and know that this too, shall pass....

Have a worshipful day!

Day 140
A REASON TO SMILE

Why should we smile and be happy?

Proverbs 17:22 A happy heart is good medicine and a cheerful mind works healing, but a broken spirit dries up the bones.

Keeping your heart happy by guarding it from evil and keeping your mind on good thoughts work wonders.

Psalm 28:7-8 The Lord is my strength and my shield; my heart trusts in, relies on, and confidently leans on him, and I am helped; therefore my heart greatly rejoices, and with my song will I praise him.

When we feel defeated, go to God for His strength and protection. Knowing that our help comes from Him, as we completely trust in Him, He gives us a wonderful reason to rejoice and to be glad.

Proverbs 15:13 A happy heart makes the face cheerful, but heartache crushes the spirit.

The joy in our hearts should show up on our face and be shared with others. Let's keep our focus on God. God's power and His righteousness live within you. That is the ultimate reason to rejoice. Let the joy of the Lord shine through you. Be a light and salt-giving flavor to the world and smile.

Have a happy day!

Day 141
YES, YOU CAN!

The key to success is God, who is with us. Moses succeeded in leading the Israelites out of Egypt because God was always with him. He then told Joshua to take up Moses' position. He told him to be strong, confident, and courageous and not afraid.

Joshua 1:5-6 No one will be able to stand up against you all the days of your life. As I was with Moses, so I will be with you; I will never leave you nor forsake you. Be strong and courageous, because you will lead these people to inherit the land I swore to their forefathers to give them.

Let us believe in God with all our trust and faith, and not rely on our own natural strength, but in God's mighty power to accomplish all things. Where we put our focus is crucial. When we look within ourselves, we limit our power and abilities, but when our focus and trust is in God, all things are possible. Don't be surprised if God asks you to fill a leadership role as well. Remember, the key is remaining in God's presence and trusting that He will never leave us. Yes, you can become all that God wants you to be.

Have a courageous day!

Day 142
A HEAVY LOAD? LEAN ON GOD

Why do we think we can handle all the stress and pressures around us? Do we really think that we are super-human? God knows that we are not and that we need Him to lean on. There is a song that goes "When there's a load you can't carry, call on me and lean on me." God wants us to do exactly that!

Psalm 91:2 I will say of the Lord, He is my Refuge and my Fortress, my God; on Him I lean and rely, and in Him I (confidently) trust!

He tells us to cast all our cares upon Him and He will sustain, strengthen, and help us! Let us come to a place of humility and release all our burdens to God, simply leaning on Him to take care of us. Don't let pride get in the way, tricking us into thinking that we can handle everything. God is here for us and when we get tired, He wants us to rest in Him.

Trust God that He is behind us and will not let us down. God promises to lift us up so that we feel that we are walking on air! Let us dwell in the midst of His Spirit today!

Have a light day!

Day 143
DOES YOUR FOCUS NEED MORE FOCUS?

Does your focus need more focus? Jackie Chan says in the movie, *Karate Kid*, "Your focus needs more focus." Think about what that means. Sometimes we think that we are focusing on the right thing, but at times we need to look beyond that which we are assuming should be a priority.

Luke 10:38-42 As Jesus and His disciples were on their way, He came to a village where a woman named Martha opened her home to Him. She had a sister called Mary, who sat at the Lord's feet listening to what he said. But Martha was distracted by all the preparations that had to be made. She came to Him and asked, "Lord, don't you care that my sister has left me to do the work by myself? Tell her to help me!" "Martha, Martha, "the Lord answered, "you are worried and upset about many things, but only one thing is needed. Mary has chosen what is better, and it will not be taken away from her."

Martha assumed her focus was correct in busying herself to prepare for Jesus, but it only upset her. Jesus loved that Mary chose to just listen and be beside Him. Let's think twice on why we are doing the things we are doing and keep our focus real and right-standing to God, which is listening and spending time with Him.

Have a better focused day!

Day 144
STEP UP, BE BOLD AND COURAGEOUS

God did not give us a spirit of fear, so let us not shrink back from it.

2 Timothy 1:7   For God did not give us a spirit of timidity (of cowardice, of craven and cringing and fawning fear), but (He has given us a spirit) of power and of love and of calm and well-balanced mind and discipline and self control.

Let us step up and be bold and courageous! Let us kneel before our God and with His power, might, and His strength. Step forward and do what is right!

Joshua 1:9   Have not I commanded you? Be strong, vigorous, and very courageous. Be not afraid, neither be dismayed, for the Lord your God is with you wherever you go.

Knowing that our Almighty God is beside us, we can take on the world! What God has called and commanded you to do, take the leap of faith and let God handle the rest. You will never have known the great blessings that you would have missed out on, if you never stepped out in boldness. Even if we feel the fear, choose to be bold and just do it in faith. Let us be encouraged to take on our opportunities with fierceness!

Have a courageous day!

Day 145
SUFFERING FOR DOING GOOD

No one enjoys suffering, but there actually is a good kind of suffering.

1 Peter 3:17 It is better, if it is God's will, to suffer for doing good than for doing evil.

When we are in the right we may suffer, but take heed, God blesses those who do good.

1 Peter 3:9 Do not repay evil with evil or insult with insult, but with blessing, because to this you were called so that you may inherit a blessing.

How easy it is when we are hurt, offended, insulted, or rejected to give payback but God tells us plainly not to retaliate but, instead, resist the natural urge to repay evil with evil. He tells us to bless them for kindness always wins. Pray for discernment. Only as believers, are we able to love, through Christ, and to yield to the Spirit of self control. When we give blessings in return for attacks of any kind, your actions of forgiveness bring blessings along with peace.

Have a yielding day!

Day 146
WHO ARE YOU NOW?

Notice at times we may see someone that we haven't seen in a while and are struck by how much their whole demeanor has changed. Their countenance looks brighter, their personality is kinder, and just about everything seems different!

Ephesians 3:16 May He grant you out of the rich treasury of His glory to be strengthened and reinforced with mighty power in the inner man by the (Holy) Spirit (Himself in dwelling in your innermost being and personality).

We give all the credit to the Holy Spirit living and activating inside of us. Day by day, the Spirit is working in you to make you more Christ-like. We know for sure that it was not by our doing! When we know who we are and whose we are with God's power and His strength, we yield to the working of the Spirit in our lives! Little by little He is changing us. We are not the same person that we used to be when we accept Christ into our hearts, and live and walk by His grace. He is definitely changing us! Let us gladly receive the compliment when someone asks us the question, "Who are you now?" Praise be to God!

Have an eager day!

Day 147
BE STEADFAST

Have you ever met anyone who no matter what happens in their life, whether they're going through struggles or not, they are just constantly steady, calm and stable? Their struggles don't seem to faze them. You would think they would overreact or jump out of their skin when bad things happen, but no, they are as stable as can be. Our enemy does not like that one bit.

James 1:4 But let endurance and steadfastness and patience have full play and do a thorough work, so that you may be perfectly and fully developed (with no defects), lacking in nothing.

As we grow in our relationship with God and know that we are His children, we find security in that alone. Eventually, we come to realize that He was with us through all of our past adversities and that He will always take care of us no matter what. "This, too, shall pass." Let us continue to build our faith and trust in Him and be steadfast. That is one way to make the enemy mad.

Have a peaceful day!

Day 148
LAUGHTER LIGHTENS THE LOAD

There is a reason why they say that laughter is the best medicine: Laughter is good for the mind, heart and soul. It helps us to not be serious all the time and it lightens our load.

Psalm 32:11   Rejoice in the Lord and be glad, you righteous; sing, all you who are upright in heart!

Notice when at times you are not able to smile or sing, a heaviness weighs down on your heart. Let us detach ourselves from the problems and find humor within it. It'll help to lighten your load and give good medicine to your body. Rejoice and be glad remembering all the goodness God has done for you, and will continue to do for you, because of His great love. Let us be encouraged to find our voice again and sing with our whole hearts. In the Swedish film, *As It Is In Heaven*, Gabriella sings, "I have never lost who I was; I have only left it sleeping." Let us awaken, rejoice, be glad and sing. Praise God with all your heart.

Have a carefree day!

Day 149
WHO ME, STUBBORN?

We wonder why at times, we can be so stubborn and want to retaliate or rebel.

Isaiah 48:8 You have neither heard nor understood; from of old your ear has not been open. Well do I know how treacherous you are; you were called a rebel from birth.

Because of our nature, we can make poor decisions and not want to obey God. The consequences are tough and disheartening!

Isaiah 48:10 See, I have refined you, though not as silver, I have tested you in the furnace of affliction.

Because of God's great love for us, He refines us to make us into a better person, even through our afflictions! The more stubborn we are to His ways, the longer we are in the rough storms of our lives. Let us take heed and surrender to His will and His ways. They are good for us!

Isaiah 48:17 This is what the Lord says-your Redeemer, the Holy One of Israel. "I am the Lord your God, who teaches you what is best for you, who directs you in the way you should go.

God personally knows us well and He knows just what it takes to refine us to His will. Trust and yield to Him today and live the extraordinary life in Him. Let go and let God take place in your life!

Have a humbling day!

Day 150
OUR OWN UNIQUE SELF

Notice in the culture we live in, we can get pressured to be like someone else rather than be our own unique self. If we buy into that idea, it can lead us towards frustrations, disappointments, rejections, and an unfulfilled lifestyle. God created us to be our own individual self with, down to our one-of-a-kind finger prints!

1 Corinthians 15:41 The sun is glorious in one way, the moon is glorious in another way, and the stars are glorious in their own (distinctive) way; for one star differs from and surpasses another in its beauty and brilliance.

When we accept ourselves on how God intricately made us, we can embrace who we really are and thrive to be used for God's glory and His purpose. Let us not compare ourselves to others, but rather be secured in who God made us to be. Let us discover and practice our gifts, talents and abilities given to us by God and Praise Him for them! Let's be encouraged to know our own worth and value in God's eyes, for we are precious to Him. Having God's Spirit living inside of us and accepting our own uniqueness, we can go far in life! Let your beauty shine with brilliance!

Have a unique day!

Day 151
RESIST EVIL AND PURSUE PEACE

The way to resist evil and pursue peace is to overcome evil with good. Let us put out any "fire" of evilness in our lives with the "water" of kindness, for fueling it with the "gasoline" of evil will continue to flame up your fire. Show non-believers what a beautiful Christian life is through your kind and gentle actions.

Romans 12:14, 16-19   Bless those who persecute you; bless and do not curse. Live in harmony with one another. Do not be proud, but be willing to associate with people of low position. Do not be conceited. Do not repay anyone evil for evil. Be careful to do what is right in the eyes of everybody. If it is possible, as far as it depends on you, live at peace with everyone. Do not take revenge, my friends, but leave room for God's wrath, for it is written: It is mine to avenge; I will repay, says the Lord.

No worries. God will handle and take care of the situation. Let's just do our part on doing what's right. True freedom is to be found in pursuing peace.

Have a right-thinking day!

Day 152
BEING A GODLY MOTHER

Mothers are very special in the eyes of God. We are able to bear children, thereby multiplying His creation, and take on the task given to us -- to raise our children well. God has given women abilities to nurture, multitask, organize and accomplish His will as mothers.

Proverbs 31:25-31 She is clothed with strength and dignity; she can laugh at the days to come. She speaks with wisdom, and faithful instruction is on her tongue. She watches over the affairs of her household and does not eat the bread of idleness. Her children arise and call her blessed; her husband also, and he praises her; Many women do noble things, but you surpass them all. Charm is deceptive, and beauty is fleeting; but a woman who fears the lord is to be praised.

We cannot go wrong when we honor and revere God, in respect for God, for He gives us the strength, courage, and wisdom to walk in His ways, to be the best mother we can be. What a privilege to be a mother and pass down our faith in God to our children. Hence, the key of being a Godly mother, is to fear and honor God in everything. Her top priority of loving and fearing the Lord gives her the strength and ability to be a Godly mother.

Have a blessed day!

Day 153
GO AND FIND OUT

When we try something new or go for unknown possibilities, all kinds of doubts, fears, suspicions and chaos could fill up our minds. God wants us to walk in complete faith in Him to go for our destinies!

Hebrew 11:8 (Urged on) by faith Abraham, when he was called, obeyed and went forth to a place which he was destined to receive as an inheritance; and he went, although he did not know or trouble his mind about where he was to go.

When or if you feel the call of God to try something new in your life, be brave enough to take even the smallest steps that head in that direction. Let us not ignore the call of God or be lazy, and miss out on our blessings. Pray and ask God to help lead and guide your steps with wisdom on how to handle situations, and to move forward in the right direction. With God's power and His strength, you can go far! Trust in Him today; you will have no regrets.

Have an enlightening day!

Day 154
GOD'S PRESENCE IS ALWAYS WITH YOU

Notice that fear can arise when dealing with unknown, challenging situations. But just imagine having and sensing the presence of mighty angels protecting you, the Holy Spirit comforting and guiding you, and the Spirit of God's surpassing peace and confidence within you!

Psalm 118:6 The Lord is with me, I will not be afraid.

See, the enemy wants us to believe the lies of negativity, and that you are alone with no one to help you, with no way out of the situation. Don't allow your mind to even go there, but right away, put your focus and attention on God and into all His promises. The sooner we do that, the better it is for us, than to dwell in anxieties and worries for who knows how long. His presence will surround you from deep within and give you a peace that is unexplainable to others. Only God can and will do that for us His children!

Let us fix our eyes upon God and let Him go to work in handling the circumstances around us. Don't give the enemy any power, but rest and rely on God's power to pull you through! Let us always magnify God rather than our problems and continue to build up our faith and trust in Him.

Have a most serene day!

Day 155
HEALING POWER IN LAUGHTER

The biological effects of laughter are good for our health; they increase blood flow and improve system response. The healing power in laughter is tremendous. Studies even show a correlation between laughter and good health.

Proverbs 17:22 A happy heart is good medicine and a cheerful mind works healing, but a broken spirit dries up the bones.

Laughter reduces stress levels and keeps us young and carefree. When you are filled with laughter, people are drawn to you. Laughter is also very contagious. Let us lighten our load with laughter.

Psalm 126:2 Our mouths were filled with laughter, our tongues with songs of joy. Then it was said among the nations, "The Lord has done great things for them.

The Lord has done great things for us, and we are filled with joy. Our joy and laughter shows how great our God is and all the great things He has done for us.

Acts 20:24 However, I consider my life worth nothing to me, if only I may finish the race and complete the task the Lord Jesus has given me -- the task of testifying to the gospel of God's grace.

Let us be encouraged to finish our course with joy. Do yourself a favor and laugh and laugh some more.

Have a healing day!

Day 156
TO BE HUMBLE

What, exactly, is the meaning of *humility*? It is knowing that God is the source of all our being. Jesus is our perfect example on how to be humble.

Philippians 2:5 Let this same attitude and purpose and (humble) mind be in you which was in Christ Jesus: (Let Him be your example in humility:)

God wants us to have humility, knowing that we cannot be, or do anything, without His strength, power and His presence. He wants all the credit that is well deserved, to dwell inside our spirit. He created you and gave you gifts, talents, and abilities. At any moment, they could all be gone.

Proverbs 15:33 The reverent and worshipful fear of the Lord brings instruction in Wisdom and humility comes before honor.

We should be encouraged to always have humility before our God in reverential fear, knowing that all our greatness comes from Him. By His love and by His grace given to us, we are who we are today.

Have a humble day!

Day 157
GOD'S SOVEREIGNTY

God has ultimate authority and He has complete control in everything!

Psalm 103:19 The Lord has established His throne in the heavens, and His kingdom rules over all.

Charles Stanley says, "When you realize that nothing happens apart from His awareness, direction, and loving purpose, it becomes possible to lay down worry and fear and truly experience His peace." With our own limited, finite minds, we are always full of questions regarding anything that don't make any sense, disasters that strike, or trials and temptations that are always lurking about. Remember God's presence and His ultimate plan and purpose for your life!

Romans 8:28 We are assured and know that all things work together and (fitting into a plan) for good to and for those who love God and are called according to (His) design and purpose.

There is always a reason why things happen. Who are we to question the Almighty God?

Hebrews 13:5-6 Never will I leave you; never will I forsake you. So we say with confidence, "The Lord is my helper; I will not be afraid. What can man do to me?

Let's stay in faith and keep trusting in Him! He has a good plan for you and for His ultimate glory! He is good!

Have a trusting day!

How is your character in the area of talking too much? Are you a gossip, or are your lips tightly sealed?

Proverbs 11:13 A gossiper betrays a confidence, but a trustworthy man keeps a secret.

Gossiping is the act of betraying someone's confidence. Have you been betrayed, or maybe you were the betrayer? Feelings of anger, sadness, and frustrations rise in these situations. God wants us to be at peace at all times.

Colossians 3:15 Let the peace of Christ rule in your hearts, since as members of one body you were called to peace. And be thankful.

Let us be responsible to be a faithful friend and a trustworthy person. Let us be encouraged to zip our lips, control our tongues, and keep information amongst you, your friend, and God.

Proverbs 10:19 The more you talk, the more likely to sin.
Psalm 141:3 Set a guard, O Lord, before my mouth; keep watch at the door of my lips.

Let us pray that the Holy Spirit will help us in wisdom, guidance and discernment in this area of our lives.

1 Peter 3:10 For let him, who wants to enjoy life and see good days, keep his tongue free from evil and his lips from guile (deceit).

Have a discerning day!

Day 159
IT'S GOOD TO BE WEAK?

In the society we live in today, we tend to get the message that we must be strong and not weak. In God's word, the message is the opposite. He says that in our own weakness, God is made strong in and through us! That may seem a little puzzling to us, but when we feel strong, we can have the attitude that we don't need any help from anyone.

2 Corinthians 12:8-10 Three times I pleaded with the Lord to take it away from me. But He said to me, "My grace is sufficient for you, for my power is made perfect in weakness." Therefore I will boast all the more gladly about my weaknesses, so that Christ's power may rest on me."That is why, for Christ's sake, I delight in weaknesses, in insults, in hardships, in persecutions, in difficulties. For when I am weak, then I am strong.

In our weaknesses, we are made aware of God's strength. He wants to show us His mighty strength, and what better way can He show this to us but through our weaknesses! When we are doing well, we tend to forget and not know the great impact of God's almighty strength. Your weakness is a gift! Let us admit our weaknesses and call unto God, allowing His divine strength to intercede on our behalf. His grace is sufficient for all our needs! Let us open our spiritual eyes and see God's strength work in and through us. Amazing things will happen! Praise God!

Have a strengthening day!

Day 160
THE NEED FOR GREATER PERSPECTIVE

It is true that certain situations call for certain measures. For example, we wouldn't sing "Happy Birthday" at a graduation party, or wear jeans and sneakers to a formal dance. There is a time and place for everything; but when it comes to praising and giving thanks to God, it is an everyday occasion!

Psalm 34:1 I will bless the Lord at all times; His praise shall continually be in my mouth.

God wants us to purposefully look within and without at all His goodness and greatness! It brings both God and us much joy when we choose to look through His perspective in our lives. We must be thankful for all that we have. It puts things into greater perspective when we see less unfortunate things that can happen to us. Instead of having a complaining attitude, let us refocus and be thankful for the small things, such as our health, eyes to see, food to taste, legs to walk, a car to drive, a workplace, family and friends, having a roof to live under, and so much more blessings than we can count.

When we change our outlook in life for the good, we can't help but to bless and praise the Lord at all times. Give it a try and see your life change for the better. It's up to us to make that choice of having nothing but praise and thanksgiving come out of our mouths! With that attitude, more blessings will come your way.

Have a delightful day!

Day 161
WHEN THINGS DON'T MAKE SENSE

God is God and we should not in any way try to figure Him out or try to reason why He does certain things.

Isaiah 55:8-9 For My thoughts are not your thoughts, neither are your ways My ways, says the Lord. For as the heavens are higher than the earth, so are My ways higher than your ways and my thoughts than your thoughts.

God created us, and who are we to try to figure out our creator? We just need to put our trust in Him and in all His ways. Trust in His perfect love for us and His perfect plan in our lives. He has a sense of humor and also likes to twist things up sometimes to keep us on our toes. Regardless, when things don't make sense, let us believe that God has everything in the palm of His hands, ready to deliver, in due time. We just need to keep our eyes fixed and focus on Him and trust in His sovereignty. Allow Him to sit at the driver's seat of our car and trust in His road map, made for each individual. He wants nothing but good for you. When we do things God's way, we are on the same page with Him, in harmony, righteousness, peace, blessedness and victory. God is one to keep His promises, even when things don't make any sense at all.

2 Samuel 7:28 And now, O Lord God, You are God, and your words are truth, and You have promised this good thing to your servant.

Have a trusting day!

Day 162
GOD OF COMFORT AND COMPASSION

When you go through the hard times in life, who do you call upon to help in times of distress? People can only do so much, but our Almighty God promises to comfort us and to have compassion on what we are going through. He knows your circumstances and heart condition so well, and so knows just what to do to help you feel His warm embrace.

Isaiah 49:13 Shout for joy, O heavens; rejoice, O earth; burst into song, O mountains! For the Lord comforts His people and will have compassion on His afflicted ones.

Call unto Him and He will help you to get out of your distress and heavy burdens. You have great worth and value to Him and He will never forget you!

Isaiah 49:16 See, I have engraved you on the palms of My hands; your walls are ever before me.

Let us trust in Him today and in His time, all things will work out for good. Let's rejoice knowing that God is here in our presence to comfort us. Thank you and praise you Lord!

Have a peaceful day!

Day 163
BE WARNED AND BEWARE

Thank goodness for God sending us His son, Jesus, to die on the cross to cleanse us from our sins. Through His bloodshed He made us well. Let us be warned and beware, we should not take advantage of God's grace and continue to intentionally sin.

John 5:14 Afterward, when Jesus found him in the temple, He said to him, See, you are well! Stop sinning or something worse may happen to you.

Continued, habitual, intentional sin leads to destruction. Be aware of whatever toxins are in your life, whether in your mind, environment, situations, etc.. and make every effort to remove yourself from them before they take a hold on you, which can be very destructive and ultimately destroy who you are as a person. Sin is a blockage in your relationship to God. They take you further away from Him and can numb your senses from hearing, seeing and sensing His presence. Pray that the Holy Spirit may help you in the area of whatever your great struggle may be in the temptation to sin. Remember, victory is ours through Christ. Live your life in freedom.

Have an aware day!

Day 164
GOD CAN AND IS ABLE TO GET OVER OUR SINS

We know full well all the mistakes and sins that we have committed in the past. How in the world are we ever to get over them? God knows because He created us, that we are not perfect and will sin repeatedly in our lifetime. That is why He sent His beloved Son Jesus to die on the cross for all of our sins: our past, present and future sins! He paid for it all to the fullest! Only through that sacrifice, God can and is able to get over our sins.

Psalm 103:8 The Lord is merciful and gracious; and full of unfailing love.

Let us realize God's precious awesome love for us. God knows the torment we will have upon ourselves and our imperfections if He was unwilling to save us from our sins.

Psalm 130:3-4 Lord, if you kept a record (grudge) of our sins, who, O Lord, could ever survive? But You offer forgiveness, that we might learn to fear you.

Some of us may have a hard time forgiving ourselves from past sins, but we just need to accept God's forgiveness offered to us and move forward in our lives. Let us confess our sins to Him and repent from it. He promises that He will forgive and forget!

Hebrews 10:17 Then He adds, 'I will never again remember their sins and lawless deeds.

He says that He will have our sins removed as far as the East is from the West. That's pretty far, so let us not be too hard on ourselves, but rather live in the freedom and love

that God offers to us. Press forward and enjoy your life!
Let us not waste Jesus precious blood from dying on the
cross for us. Instead, let us be grateful and value His
sacrifice for us all!

Have a humbling day!

Day 165
ARISE FROM YOUR DEPRESSION!

During times of depression, defeat, and despair, we must vigilant and disallow the enemy to take the best of us. Every moment we spend feeling down and out builds up a stronghold in depression. Stand firm, be bold and courageous, and keep God's strength and might within you, mustering up all your faith, believing that God will pull you out of despair.

Isaiah 60:1 Arise (from the depression and prostration in which circumstances have kept you -- rise to a new life)! Shine (be radiant with the glory of the Lord), for your light has come, and the glory of the Lord has risen upon you.

God is telling us, "Enough is enough." Arise now from your depressed condition.

Exodus 14:14 The Lord will fight for you, and you shall hold your peace and remain at rest.

Believe that being a child of God, He loves you and will take care of you.

Isaiah 58:8 Then shall your light break forth like the morning, and your healing shall spring forth speedily; your righteousness shall go before you, and the glory of the Lord shall be your rear guard.

We need to take that first step, believing that all will be well. Trust in God and keep on trusting in Him.

Have an awakening day!

THE KEY TO SEEING GOD

How's your heart condition lately? If you feel a little distant towards God and cannot sense His presence, then it may be due to a heart that has become cluttered or calloused with the lies and distractions of the world. Our flesh loves to take over and all kinds of selfishness, ugly thoughts, wrong behaviors, etc., can corrupt our hearts without us even realizing it! We can wonder to ourselves, "Where is God?"

Matthew 5:8 Blessed are the pure in heart, for they will see God.

When we ask God to help us to cleanse our heart through His Holy Spirit and renew our soul to be pure, we are able to see God crystal clear. We can see and feel His presence in everything and in every way! Let us keep our heart in check and stay away from evil.

Proverbs 4:23 Above all else, guard your heart, for it is the wellspring of life.

It's a guarantee that with a pure heart, we can truly see God. Our spiritual eyes are wide open! Let us pray that God will soften our hearts today to draw closer to Him. Let us receive the key to seeing God and use it for His glory!

Have a purifying day!

Day 167
GOD'S STRENGTH MADE PERFECT IN OUR WEAKNESS

Have you ever had those times when you felt completely exhausted and tired and you felt that you couldn't go on any longer for even a single moment? Yet, you were able to keep on going for God's supernatural divine strength intervened.

Isaiah 40:29 He gives power to the faint and weary, and to him who has no might He increases strength (causing it to multiply and making it to abound).

Thank goodness when God sees that we need more strength, at our lowest point of weariness, He provides and multiplies it for us.

2 Corinthians 12:9 But He said to me, "My grace is sufficient for you, for my power is made perfect in weakness. Therefore I will boast all the more gladly about my weakness, so that Christ's power may rest on me. That is why, for Christ's sake, I delight in weakness, in insults, in hardships, in persecutions, in difficulties. For when I am weak, then I am strong.

Even in and through our weaknesses, let's see them as opportunities for God's strength to manifest in us and give Him all praise and glory. Then you can truly see God's power and His greatness.

Have a strong day!

Day 168
WHERE'S YOUR COMPASSION?

To have understanding and to have compassion for others goes hand in hand. It is by far too easy to judge others, rather than have mercy or compassion on them. When we try to imagine putting ourselves in others' shoes, we might get a glimpse of why they do what they do.

Matthew 9:36 When He saw the crowds, He had compassion on them, because they were harassed and helpless, like sheep without a shepherd.

In one way or another, we are all lost. God tells us to have compassion and to love one another!

John 13:34 I give you a new commandment: that you should love one another. Just as I have loved you, so you too should love one another.

God gives us a perfect example on how we are to treat others. How are we to love others without having compassion first? We should treat others the way we want to be treated. Be kind and compassionate, letting God's Spirit go to work within you.

Have a kind day!

Day 169
GOD KNOWS US SO WELL

Have you ever wished or yearned for someone to just understand you and where you're coming from? God knows us better than we know ourselves.

Psalm 139:1-4 O Lord, you have searched me (thoroughly) and have known me. You know my down sitting and my uprising; You understand my thought afar off. You sift and search out my path and my lying down, and You are acquainted with all my ways. For there is not a word in my tongue (still unuttered), but, behold, O Lord, you know it altogether.

Wow! How personalized is that! God is so intimate with us and knows us so well! People can judge us and think that they have us all figured out, but they cannot see our heart!

1 Samuel 16:7 But the Lord said to Samuel, "Look not on his appearance or at the height of his stature, for I have rejected him. For the Lord sees not as man sees; for man looks on the outward appearance, but the Lord looks on his heart.

Our main concern should be our heart condition. That is where our source should be! Our attitude, behaviors and actions follows from our heart. Let us pray that our God, who knows us so well, will help us to work on our heart to be good, pure and pleasing to Him! Trust in Him to know just what to do for you.

Have a heart-happy day!

Day 170
GO WITH GOD'S AGENDA

God has an agenda: to fulfill His purpose in you and in your life. See what happens when we look to God in times of need.

Psalm 55:22 Cast your burden on the Lord (releasing the weight of it) and He will sustain you; He will never allow the (consistently) righteous to be moved (made to slip, fall, or fail).

God does not want us to take on our burdens by ourselves. Release them to God.

Psalm 57:2 I will cry to God Most High, Who performs on my behalf and rewards me (Who brings to pass His purposes for me and surely completes them)! Sooner or later, God is going to have His way with you and help you, but you need to first cast your burdens to Him and cry out to Him. The sooner you choose to look to Him, your purposes will be done. Go with God's agenda and trust in Him today to fulfill your purpose in your life, whatever it may be. He will help direct you in His good plan.

Have a yielding day!

Day 171
PEACE IS PRICELESS

In life's tough situations, ask yourself the question, "Is it worth it to lose our peace?" Peace is priceless and whatever the situation may be, it is definitely not worth losing it.

2 Thessalonians 3:16   Now may the Lord of peace himself grant you His peace (the peace of His kingdom) at all times and in all ways (under all circumstances and conditions, whatever comes). The Lord (be) with you all.

It is very easy to stir up negative emotions, thoughts, and actions if we don't keep a check on the challenges that arise in life. It can also cause us to lose our peace and joy. It is vital that we go to God, first and foremost, and ask for peace, and to remain there. The enemy loves to throw us off track in our walk with God and distract us by whatever means and pull us away from Him. Fight and don't allow that to happen. If we give into his ways, it opens the door to frustrations, disappointments, and animosities. We have to nip it in the bud before it can get out of control.

Proverbs 3:5-6   Trust in the Lord with all your heart and lean not on your own understanding; in all your ways acknowledge Him, and He will make your paths straight.

When we keep our eyes focused on God, He makes everything which seems impossible, possible.

Have a peaceful day!

Day 172
EXPERIENCE JOY AS A CALM DELIGHT

When we think of the word "joy" we may think that it means to be happy and excited all the time. But in reality, that feeling may just come once in a while, regarding our circumstances.

John 15:11 I have told you these things, that My joy and delight may be in you, and that your joy and gladness may be of full measure and complete and overflowing.

Strong's Concordance defines joy as a "calm delight." Now, in reality, we can do just that! An inner calmness with peace, and delight in your heart whether you have a good day or a bad day! God wants us to know that His joy and delight resides within us! He desires us to use His joy up so that it may be complete and overflowing in our lives. Let us go the extra mile on allowing our joy to overflow, by guarding our hearts from evil and praising God with all our mind, heart and soul! Even in the midst of hard times, having the assurance of God's presence, gives us the inner peace of a calm delight.

Have a delightful day!

Day 173
WHAT DO I REALLY NEED?

If someone was to ask you to make a list of all the things that you need, it may surprise you to see from what you wrote down, what God's list may be for you!

Matthew 6:7-8 And when you pray, do not keep on babbling like pagans, for they think they will be heard because of their many words. Do not be like them, for your Father knows what you need before you ask Him.

God knows you so well that He already knows what you need! Sometimes, the things that we think we need, God sees something entirely different. Do we need some humility, some mercy or compassion? How about more trust in God? It's like a child telling his parents, "Mom and dad, I need this and I need that," but as parents we know what they *really* need. We give them what they want and what they can handle at that point in their lives. God graciously gives us what we need before and after we ask Him. We do not have to repeat ourselves over and over again. Trust in His wisdom and care for you. It may surprise you, what you thought you wanted is not truly what you needed!

Have a thought-provoking day!

Day 174
LIFE CAN BE A SURPRISE

Isn't it astonishing how the plans we make can change in an instant? Anything can come about to change what we had in store. We may get an urgent phone call, we can get sick, or others can cancel on us. Let us learn to live and enjoy each day, a day at a time.

James 4:13-15 Now listen, you who say, "Today or tomorrow we will go to this or that city, spend a year there, carry on business and make money." Why, you do not even know what will happen tomorrow. What is your life? You are a mist that appears for a little while and then vanishes. Instead, you ought to say, "If it is the Lord's will, we will live and do this or that."

We should not boast for tomorrow, for we never know what may happen. Let us be in line with God's will every day. We may encounter better opportunities that are in God's plan for us without even realizing it. Life can be a surprise in many ways so let us enjoy each day to the fullest.

Have a good day!

Day 175
BE KIND AND SENSITIVE

Did you know that we have the capacity to be a hindrance or a stumbling block for another person's walk with God?

Romans 14:13 Therefore let us stop passing judgment on one another. Instead, make up your mind not to put any stumbling block or obstacle in your brother's way.

Let us who are strong, put others before ourselves and help the weak!

Romans 15:1-2 We who are strong ought to bear with the failings of the weak and not to please ourselves. Each of us should please his neighbor for his good, to build him up.

Now, we do have the capacity to help, encourage, edify, strengthen and make happy our neighbor in Christ! A part of our walk with God is for us to live in mutual harmony, sympathy and unity with one another.

Romans 15:5 May the God Who gives endurance and encouragement give you a spirit of unity among yourselves as you follow Christ Jesus.

Let us pray that God's spirit will help us to see people through His loving eyes. We can be the one who can take part into helping others grow in God's kingdom through His love! Let us do good for the goodness of doing good. Be kind and sensitive to others. Tap into your kindness bank and give out lavishly!

Have a kind and giving day!

Day 176
LIFE PURPOSEFULLY AND WORTHILY

There should be a good reason why we do the things we do. Our motives, intentions, and purposes should be aligned with God's. Let us be fruitful in all our ways, honoring God in everything.

Ephesians 5:15-17 Look carefully then how you walk! Live purposefully and worthily and accurately, not as the unwise and witless, but as wise (sensible, intelligent people). Making the very most of the time (buying up each opportunity), because the days are evil. Therefore do not be vague and thoughtless and foolish, but understanding and firmly grasping what the will of the Lord is.

God does not want us to waste our time and energy on the senseless, foolish things of the world. Instead, He wants us to grow, excel and prosper for His kingdom. As we are in the positions of being a child of God, a parent, an employee, a friend, a spouse, etc.., let us be our best that we can be whilst using wisdom, paying attention to our roles with great purpose and fulfillment. Let us be encouraged to be productive in all our ways and make an impact wherever we are.

Have a fruitful day!

Day 177
WOUNDED AND BROKEN HEARTED?

I am sure at one time or another we have had a broken and wounded heart. It may have been in our childhood, or from our family and friends, or in many unfortunate situations in life that just seemed unfair to us. Let us be open and invite Jesus to heal us and set us free!

Isaiah 61:1 The Spirit of the Sovereign Lord is on me, because the Lord has anointed me to preach good news to the poor, He has sent me to bind up the brokenhearted, to proclaim freedom for the captives and release from darkness for the prisoners.

God's desire is to heal and restore your heart to be whole and free! Sometimes being repeatedly wounded, we can become numb in wanting to get well and we find comfort in where we are at. But there is so much out there in life to enjoy, such as living in beauty, gladness, praise and in righteousness!

Isaiah 61:3 ...and provide for those who grieve in Zion- to bestow on them a crown of beauty instead of ashes, the oil of gladness instead of mourning, and a garment of praise instead of a spirit of despair. They will be called oaks of righteousness, a planting of the Lord for the display of His splendor.

Pray that God will heal your wounded heart and release you from darkness into His light. Trust in Him today to work on your heart to be made well, whole and new!

Have a liberating day!

Day 178
SET YOUR MINDS AND KEEP THEM SET

Notice the word, *set*, means to place something. God always wants us to set our minds on Him and on things above.

Colossians 3:2 And set your minds and keep them set on what is above (the higher things), not on the things that are on the earth.

God must have known that if we set our minds on earthly things, chaos and disappointments can fill our minds and bring us down. They can all lead toward depressions and destruction. To be in constant peace, hope and joy, we must train ourselves to set our minds on good and higher things above. When we don't keep our minds on God and on His ways, our minds can easily drift around being flighty and unstable. It also easily opens the door for the enemy to attack. The importance of keeping our mind set on Him and what is good is crucial to living a life of victory.

Philippians 4:8 Finally, brothers, whatever is true, whatever is noble, whatever is right, whatever is pure, whatever is lovely, whatever is admirable -- if anything is excellent or praiseworthy -- think about such things.

Remember, where the mind goes, behavior and actions follow.

Have a good-focused day!

Day 179
PRECIOUS TREASURE WITHIN

Do you realize that you have a precious treasure within you? God wants us to shine forth His light of this treasure, of His power, to others.

2 Corinthians 4:6-7 For God Who said, Let light shine out of darkness, has shone in our hearts so as (to beam forth) the Light for the illumination of the knowledge of the majesty and glory of God (as it is manifest in the Person and is revealed) in the face of Jesus Christ. However, we possess this precious treasure (the divine Light of the Gospel) in (frail human) vessels of earth, that the grandeur and exceeding greatness of the power may be shown to be from God and not from ourselves.

We are God's representatives here on earth and He wants His power and glory to shine in us and through us to others! We are the vessels of His light. As believers, we have the privilege of having God's precious treasure within us. Let His power manifest, shine and bring glory to all.

Have a beautiful day!

Day 180
HOW'S YOUR BALANCE LATELY?

The importance of staying balanced in your life is crucial. Once we get off-balance, the enemy is right there to get us off track with our walk with God, and devour without us even realizing it.

1 Peter 5:8 Be well balanced (temperate, sober of mind), be vigilant and cautious at all times; for that enemy of yours, the devil, roams around like a lion roaring (in fierce hunger), seeking someone to seize upon and devour.

The main key to keeping our balance is to fix our eyes on God and stay focused on Him. Ask Him to help you to stay in balance. If you feel that you are excessively focusing or using all your energy in one area and neglecting other areas that need your attention, then refocus and be sensitive to the Spirit's leading. Too much of work, play, rest, spending money, talking, etc., can get you off-balance. A person walking on a tightrope has to stay focused on a stable object ahead of him to keep in balance. Otherwise, he can easily fall off the tightrope and will fall! Jesus is our focus and He is our stability. Pray that He will help you to have a healthy, well-balanced mind and life! That way we will not be easy prey for the enemy to make us fall.

Have a well-balanced day!

Day 181
CHECK YOURSELVES WHEN FRUSTRATED

Notice how frustrations come about when things don't go our way, when we can't handle certain matters, when disappointment within ourselves arises, or even when we get expectations from others? They all come from our fleshly ways. The job of the Holy Spirit for us believers is to help us grow into perfection or maturity. It is a process we make in our life journey.

Galatians 3:3 Are you so foolish and so senseless and so silly? Having begun (your new life spiritually) with the (Holy) Spirit, are you now reaching perfection (by dependence) on the flesh?

We must be patient with ourselves, trusting in God's timing to help us with the power of His Spirit to be more Christ-like in our character living the good life in Him. Let us learn to depend on the spirit in times of need, rather than trying to do everything ourselves, which leads towards frustrations. Pray and believe that the Spirit will help make you anew each and every day!

Have a growing day!

Day 182
WOW, WHAT A CONTRAST

Talk about an extreme difference! God's purpose in our life is to be transformed. Most of us are not comfortable with who and where we are in life. That's why there are so many complaints! God has a much greater plan to transform us to be Christ like. It may seem impossible, but when we come to realize who we are through His Holy Spirit living inside of us, it is a great possibility! As we cooperate with His Spirit and surrender to God, great changes take place.

Ephesians 4:31-31 Get rid of all bitterness, rage and anger, brawling and slander, along with every form of malice. Be kind and compassionate to one another, forgiving each other, just as Christ forgave you.

The more we resist God's attempts to lead us to change and transform (make us new) through Him, the more we will be stagnant and never experience the magnificent, abundant, blessed life intended for us.

Romans 8:29 For those whom He foreknew, He also destined from the beginning to be molded into the image of His Son (and share inwardly His likeness), that He might become the firstborn among many brethren.

Let's take up the challenge to be transformed into Christ's likeness, trusting in God, our potter, making and molding us every day! God desires what is good for us! He'll do whatever is necessary to bring transformation in our thought life, attitudes, actions, and priorities. True freedom, peace, and joy is found in Christ and being Christ like!

Have a transforming day!

Day 183
EVERYTHING IS GOING TO BE FINE

Have you noticed that when life is good, sooner or later, trials and distress of some kind seem to follow? That is what we call life. Jesus tells us not to worry for He has already overcome the world.

John 16:33 I have told you these things, so that in Me you may have (perfect) peace and confidence. In the world you have tribulation and trials and distress and frustration; but be of good cheer (take courage, be confident, certain, undaunted)! For I have overcome the world. (I have deprived it of power to harm you and have conquered it for you).

It can't get any better than that, for victory is ours through Jesus Christ. We see God through Jesus, who is in us.

John 17:26 I have made your name known to them and revealed your character and your very self, and I will continue to make (You) known, that the love which You have bestowed upon Me may be in them (felt in their hearts) and that I (Myself) may be in them.

Jesus is alive and well, living inside all of us. Therefore, we have His might and His power to conquer anything and everything we encounter. Praise God! Let us believe that we are already made conquerors through Him.

Have a victorious day!

Day 184
HOW DO YOU COMPARE?

How easy is it to compare ourselves with others! Whether it is by our looks, possessions, positions, families, or capabilities, our human nature has a natural tendency to want to compare.

Galatians 6:4 Each one should test his own actions. Then he can take pride in himself, without comparing himself to somebody else.

How tempting it is to always compare ourselves to the earthly things! How about comparing ourselves to Jesus instead of the people and the things on earth?

Colossians 3:1-2 Since, then, you have been raised with Christ, set your heart on things above, where Christ is seated at the right hand of God. Set your minds on things above, Not on earthly things.

Let us compare ourselves to Jesus characteristics, His abilities, His poise, power and strength, etc.. As believers, we already have all of those attributes within us. We just have to activate them with the power of His Spirit. The higher things from above are worth comparing to, because that is where our mindset should be in order to stay in good health, peace and happiness. When you find yourselves comparing to others, choose instead to compare with Jesus because that itself is attainable!

Have a right-comparison day!

Day 185
LITTLE THINGS DO MATTER

We have all heard, "That doesn't matter," or "It's no big deal," many times in our lives. Those are the times when we must be vigilant against attacks from the enemy. Little annoyances, disappointments, frustrations, anger, etc.. always start out small, but in time, as they build and enlarge, they can turn into gigantic problems.

Song of Solomon 2:15 Catch us the foxes, the little foxes that spoil the vines, for our vines have tender grapes.

Let us be aware and be very careful to watch out for those little foxes that can destroy friendships, marriages, work situations, etc.. Pray that God will help you take care of the small matters before they get out of control.

Have a discerning day!

Day 186
EXPRESS YOUR SPECIAL THANKS

Thanksgiving reminds us to think about all our blessings throughout the year. But this is something we can do daily! Try humbly writing down or expressing your gratitude with a grateful heart, and all of God's good gifts and blessings, big and small, will amaze you.

Psalm 103:1-2 Bless (affectionately, gratefully praise) the Lord, O my soul; and all that is (deepest) within me, bless His Holy name! Bless the Lord, O my soul, and forget not (one of) all his benefits.

God wants us to adoringly express all of our deepest blessings to Him. Let us not forget who He is, and what He does for us. He forgives us, heals us, redeems our life from the pit and corruption, and beautifies us with loving kindness and tender mercy. God provides us with family, friends, and a one-of-a-kind life. Wow! It sounds like God is busy in His business of blessing us!

I encourage you to constantly remember the real purpose of Thanksgiving and express your special thanks to God. He'll have a big smile on His face. Imagine that! He deserves all our praise.

Have a beautiful day!

Day 187
NO ONE IS EXCLUDED FROM GOD'S USE AND HIS GLORY

There may be some of us who think that God will never use them for His kingdom's work. Do not be hard on yourself for God knows you so well and He will pour out abundantly His grace and mercy on you to do His will.

1 Timothy 1:12-14 I thank Christ Jesus our Lord, who has given me strength, that He considered me faithful, appointing me to His service. Even though I was once s blasphemer and a persecutor and a violent man, I was shown mercy because I acted in ignorance and unbelief. The grace of our Lord was poured out on me abundantly, along with the faith and love that are in Christ Jesus.

Paul was a wretc.hed man. Yet, God used him in a mighty way. No one is excluded for God's use and His Glory. Let us be open and willing to be used by God. Don't give up on yourself. God has a great and wonderful plan just for you. Receive God's love for you today.

Have a purposeful day!

Day 188
DON'T BECOME LAZY IN DOING GOOD

How often we like to see immediate results when we work on things; we like to be and feel productive instantly! God's time line can be very different from ours. He sees and notices every good work you do for Him. He won't forget one single thing you did and do in honor of Him.

Hebrews 6:10 God is not unjust; He will not forget your work and the love you have shown Him as you have helped His people and continue to help them. We want each of you to show this same diligence to the very end, in order to make your hope sure. We do not want you to become lazy, but to imitate those who through faith and patience inherit what has been promised.

At times you may feel discouraged, defeated, or just plain tired of not seeing any results when you put in all your efforts in doing good and helping others. Don't give up! God is faithful with His promises to you.

Hebrews 6:13-15 When God made His promise to Abraham, since there was no one greater for him to swear by, He swore Himself, saying, "I will surely bless you and give you many descendants." And so after waiting patiently, Abraham received what was promised.

May we do good and live authentically for the glory of God!

Have a productive day!

Day 189
PUT ON THE EFFORT

God has chosen us to be His representatives here on earth and He wants us to daily put on the effort of clothing ourselves in the behavior of His ways of gentleness, patience, and long suffering.

Colossians 3:12 Clothe yourselves therefore, as God's own chosen ones (His own picked representatives), (who are) purified and holy and well-beloved (by God Himself, by putting on behavior marked by) tenderhearted pity and mercy, kind feeling, a lowly opinion of yourselves, gentle ways, patience (which is tireless and long suffering, and has the power to endure whatever comes, with good temper).

These behaviors go against our natural human tendencies. God must have known that it can be a great challenge at times, so therefore, He literally tells us, His children, to make the conscious effort daily to put on the clothing of these behaviors. He knows, ultimately, it is for our own good and for the good of others. Putting on these behaviors ties in together with love and peace, being thankful to God, and giving Him all praise.

Have an awareness day!

Day 190
HOW'S YOUR SPEECH?

How easy it can be to automatically judge someone by the way they talk and what they talk about.

James 3:8-10 But no man can tame the tongue. It is a restless evil, full of deadly poison. With the tongue we praise our Lord and Father, and with it we curse men, who have been made in God's likeness. Out of the same mouth come praise and cursing. My brothers, this should not be.

What is in your heart comes out in your speech. God does not want us to speak of evil and good from the same mouth. He wants our thoughts and hearts to be in agreement with His love and wisdom!

James 3:17 But the wisdom from above is first of all pure; then it is peace-loving, courteous (considerate, gentle). (It is willing to) yield to reason, full of compassion and good fruits; it is wholehearted and straightforward, impartial and unfeigned (free from doubts, wavering, and insincerity).

The power of your tongue can bring blessings or curses.

Psalm 141:3 Set a guard, O Lord, before my mouth; keep watch at the door of my lips.

We build our character as we learn to control our tongue. Let only what's good, edifying and pleasing to God come out of our mouths. Blessings will come!

Have a wise day!

Day 191
LET PEACE BE YOUR GUIDE

What do you do when you have a decision you have to make, whether it big or small? God wants us to let peace be our guide.

Colossians 3:15 And let the peace (soul harmony which comes) from Christ rule (act as umpire continually) in your hearts (deciding and settling with finality all questions that arise in your minds, in that peaceful state) to which as one body you were also called (to live). And be thankful, (giving praise to God always).

Making certain decisions can leave us with confusion. Also, because we want to make the right choice, it can also leave us with uncertainty. When we want to do things our own way, with no regard to God's will, chaos abounds. The umpire in a baseball game tells you whether or not the ball is in. That is how peace should operate in our lives. Pray for wisdom and guidance along with God's peace to direct you in the ways you should go.

If you have already made certain choices with uneasiness and discomfort, then pray today that you will be led by peace by keeping your eyes fixed on God. Following the guidance of peace gives us a rich, blessed and abundant life in Christ.

Have a peaceful day!

Day 192
REMEMBER, THIS TOO SHALL PASS

Are you going through a difficult and challenging time right now in your life? Remember, this too shall pass. Think about all the hard times you went through in the past; I'm sure when you were going through those hard times, you may have thought to yourself that you were always going to stay there and never be able to get through those challenges! Thank goodness with time and the help of God's strength and His grace, you were able to get past those hardships!

2 Corinthians 4:17-18 For our light and momentary troubles are achieving for us an eternal glory that far outweighs them all. So we fix our eyes not on what is seen, but what is unseen. For what is seen is temporary, but what is unseen is eternal.

In and through your own personalized trials, God is faithful and will never leave you! When trials seem to stay with you, remind yourself to do what is good and right. Don't go in your own ways and do what seems natural, listening to the lies of the enemy and making wrong choices! Instead, put your hope and faith in God and remember His great love for you! God is always preparing us and He wants His glory to outshine in and through our lives!

Have an enduring day!

Day 193
THE JOY OF SERVING

Have you become best friends with three people named me, myself, and I? It is hard to get away from ourselves and we constantly succumb to vanity and conceit. But there is a way that *we* can be honored by God!

John12:25-26 If anyone serves Me, he must continue to follow Me (to cleave steadfastly to Me, conform wholly to My example in living and, if need be, in dying) and wherever I am, there will My servant be also. If anyone serves me, the Father will honor him.

God intended every believer to be a servant. The attitude of a servant gets you far in life!

1 Peter 4:10 Each one should use whatever gift he has received to serve others, faithfully administering God's grace in its various forms.

Everything changes when we have an attitude of servant hood. We become united in Christ as our example, to live our lives serving others as He has. The joy and beauty of seeing people serve with a humble and pure heart is glorious and God surely honors that!

Proverbs 22:4 The reward of humility and the reverent and worshipful fear of the Lord is riches and honor and life.

Let's be encouraged to take on the spirit and attitude of a servant. It surely is a winner in God's eyes!

Have a serving day!

Day 194
WHERE DO YOU PLACE YOUR FEAR?

Why is it that we can get so caught up and afraid of what man can do to us? God created man and He alone has all power over them.

Psalm 56:3-4 What time I am afraid, I will have confidence in and put my trust and reliance in You. By (the help of) God I will praise His word; on God I lean, rely, and confidently put my trust; I will not fear. What can man, who is flesh, do to me?

Let us use our will to choose, to do, what is right. Let us go beyond our feelings, fears, anxieties, and worries and put our trust in Almighty God. He has your back and He will make all things work out according to His plan and His good purpose. Let us put our reverential fear in God and in Him alone; that is where true peace is found.

Have a good day!

Day 195
REWARDS OF PROSPERITY BY OUR OBEDIENCE

People give orders for a specific reason. God has given us an order for our own good and to prosper us in all that we do.

Deuteronomy 30:9-11 Then the Lord your God will make you prosperous in all the work of your hands and in the fruit of your womb, the young of your livestock and the crops of your land. The Lord will again delight in you and make you prosperous, just as He delighted in your fathers, if you obey the Lord your God and keep His commands and degrees that are written in His Book of the Law and turn to the Lord your God with all your heart and with all your soul.

What great rewards are given to prosper us in everything if we simply obey God wholeheartedly! Our love for God should be shown by our obedience to Him. As parents lovingly care for their own children and have abundant gifts and blessings in store for them, they watch how they obey their parents' commands in love. One way to strengthen a relationship is through acts of love and obedience. Let us be encouraged to grow in our relationship with God our Father.

Have a blessed day!

Day 196
HOLD YOUR GROUND! DO NOT BE
INTIMIDATED

Have you ever been intimidated by a bully? The enemies in your life can be things that put you in fear, such as financial struggles, bad health, challenging relationships, or any other kind of giants that can make you feel intimidated and in defeat.

Philippians 1:28 And do not (for a moment) be frightened or intimidated in anything by your opponents and adversaries, for such (constancy and fearlessness) will be a clear sign (proof and seal) to them of destruction, but (a sure token and evidence) of your deliverance and salvation, and that from God.

The enemy loves to threaten us, but it is only a threat. We are more than conquerors with God on our side. We have the power to defeat and overcome the enemy by staying constant and fearless! Remember, our oppositions bring promotion!

Exodus 1:12 But the more they were oppressed, the more they multiplied and spread.

Let us look forward to the victories and glory of God in increase as we stay in faith, confidence and fearlessness! That for sure will weaken the power of the enemies in our lives.

Have a confident day!

Day 197
COME TO YOUR SENSES

Is anyone at a place of brokenness? God wants us to come to Him, to come to our senses and realize who we are, children of Him. Brokenness leads to blessedness.

Luke 15:19-20,24 I am no longer worthy to be called your son; (just) make me like one of your hired servants. So he got up and came to his (own) father. But while he was still a long way off, his father saw him and was moved with pity and tenderness (for him); and he ran and embraced him and kissed him (fervently). Because this my son was dead and is alive again; he was lost and is found! And they began to revel and feast and make merry.

It doesn't matter to God, our Father, what we have done in the past or where we have been. All He wants is for us to repent and turn to Him for His love, acceptance, and forgiveness. Once we come to our senses and remember that we are His children, God runs to us and embraces us and lavishly loves and fulfills us with everything He has. Let us experience the abundant life found as God's own children. Feel God's loving embrace today.

Have a beautiful day!

Day 198
DOES ANYONE UNDERSTAND ME?

Have you ever felt that nobody understands you and all that you go through in your life? You may wonder if they genuinely care about you and your hurts, temptations, and trials that you face. Jesus completely understands you and He knows exactly what you are going through!

Hebrews 4:15 For we do not have a High Priest Who is unable to understand and sympathize and have a shared feeling with our weakness and infirmities and liability to the assaults of temptation, but One Who has been tempted in every respect as we are, yet without sinning.

Let us trust in Jesus and go to Him for help, comfort, sympathy, and encouragement. He wants to connect with you! Allow Him to walk with you through the process of healing. He'll know exactly what you need and He'll know what to do to comfort you! You are not alone. Let Him be your friend and comforter.

Have a peaceful day!

Day 199
THE CHALLENGE OF LISTENING

When a person assumes certain things, or comes to his or her own conclusions, this can lead towards anger. Maybe the problem lies with not being a good listener! God wants us to listen first and foremost thoroughly, then speak with wisdom, and be slow to anger if necessary.

James 1:19 Understand (this) my beloved brethren. Let every man be quick to hear (a ready listener), slow to speak, slow to take offense and to get angry.

Try the best you can not to become angry. There is always a reason people do and say certain things and by hearing their story with compassion, it can change the way you see and feel about them! Allow the Spirit to lead and guide you in this manner. It can be a challenge to bite our tongues and listen without putting in our own "two cents." The more we practice this good habit, the more of a righteous life we can live in favor with God.

James 1:20 For man's anger does not promote the righteousness God (wishes and requires).

Have a discerning day!

Day 200
WE HAVE THE MIND OF CHRIST

Do we have the mind of Christ? How in the world can we have Jesus' mind, heart, attitude and behavior?

1 Corinthians 2:16 "For who has known the mind of the Lord that he may instruct him?" But we have the mind of Christ.

It says clearly that as believers, we have Christ's mind in us through His Holy Spirit.

1 Corinthians 2:10-13 but God has revealed it to us by His Spirit. The Spirit searches all things of God. For who among men knows the thoughts of a man except the man's spirit within him? In the same way no one knows the thoughts of God except the spirit of God. We have not received the Spirit of the world but the Spirit who is from God, that we may understand what God has freely given us. This is what we speak, not in words taught us by human wisdom but in words taught by the Spirit, expressing spiritual truths in spiritual words.

The key here is that the Holy Spirit knows God's mind and we have His Spirit living inside of us, given to us after Jesus' resurrection. We need to plug into His Spirit and daily activate it through our lives to see everything through God's perspective. Let us be encouraged to yield to God's Spirit day by day and have Christ's mind to help us in our daily lives. His way of thinking leads to peace, joy, and happiness.

Have a wonderful day!

Day 201
BECOME EFFORTLESS IN YOUR GRATITUDE

Saying "Thank You," should be effortless. If it is hard for you to be thankful, then do not be surprised if you are unhappy. The power and atmosphere that is created by a thankful heart is very important! We all like to be appreciated by all the kind and good things that we do. Imagine how God delights in us as we constantly and effortlessly give Him thanks and praise.

1 Chronicles 16:34   O give thanks to the Lord, for He is good; for His mercy and loving-kindness endure forever!

Think of *all* the big and small things that you are thankful for and surprise yourself with the list that you created in your mind and heart. To be in appreciation and gratitude always puts you in a good spirit! God is always faithful, kind and good to us, and forever will be! Let's give Him the thanks that He deserves. Praise God!

Have the most thankful day!

Day 202
IT ALL STARTS WITH YOUR MIND

I think one of the most fascinating and greatest powers we have within our human bodies is our mind. It controls every aspect of our being such as our attitudes, feelings, behaviors, actions and goals. How we chose to think, greatly affects you today.

Romans 12:2 Do not be transformed to this world, (fashioned after and adapted to its external, superficial customs), but be transformed (changed) by the (entire) renewal of your mind (by its new ideals and its new attitude), so that you may prove what is the good and acceptable and perfect will of God, even the thing which is good and acceptable and perfect (in His sight for you).

Allow God's Spirit to control your thoughts to be aligned with God's word and His will for you. You will then have God's discernment and His perspective in every matter and this will lead you in the right direction of everything good. Let us guard and protect our minds from the world's ideas and fashions, and be transformed when we surrender to God.

Ephesians 4:23 And be constantly renewed in the spirit of your mind (having a fresh mental and spiritual attitude). And put on the new nature created in God's image, (Godlike) in true righteousness and holiness.

Let us be renewed by God's word day by day for peace, love, freedom and victory.

Have a beautiful day!

Day 203
IT'S NOT ALL THAT BAD, BUT MAY BE GOOD

Sometimes we may go through hard challenges and trials that appear to be a default in our lives. Don't be surprised if many good things come out from these seemingly 'bad' experiences. God can work in ways that you will never expect.

Philippians 1:12 Now I want you to know and continue to rest assured, brethren, that what (has happened) to me (this imprisonment) has actually only served to advance and give a renewed impetus to the (spreading of the) good news (the Gospel).

The fact that Paul was in prison did not stop him from spreading the Good News. If we are open and willing to be used by God, let us trust in His ways to go about His plans for our lives!

Philippians 1:6 And I am convinced and sure of this very thing, that He Who began a good work in you will continue until the day of Jesus Christ, developing (that good work) and perfecting and bringing it to full completion in you.

So, when things seem really bad, it just may be the stepping stone for an ultimate good! Let us put our hope and trust in God for all things will work out according to His plan for those who love Him.

Have a hopeful day!

Day 204
DON'T STAND ALONE

What does *faith* mean exactly? God wants us to put our faith in Him and in Him alone. He wants our whole being to trust in Him.

Colossians 1:4 For we have heard of your faith in Christ Jesus (the leaning of your entire human personality on Him in absolute trust and confidence in His power, wisdom, and goodness) and of the love which you (have and show) for all the saints (God's consecrated ones).

Don't allow yourself to stand alone. That only brings pressure and can be very lonely. Lean on God entirely and put your rest, confidence, and trust in Him. Our good God will give you the strength and power you need, with His guidance, knowledge and wisdom for everything that is good for you. As we lean on a wall or sit on a chair, that is how God wants our rest and faith to be placed on Him. Put all your weight on God. That is how we build our faith in Him.

Have a weightless day!

Day 205
IT'S AS SIMPLE AS HOPE

When we truly believe who our almighty God is and in His character, we can't help but to have hope in our lives in every situation.

Matthew 19:26 But Jesus looked at them and said, With men this is impossible, but all things are possible with God.

Not a few selective things, but all things! The meaning of hope is "an inkling of a glimpse of anything good from a bad situation." There is great power in the word hope. Receive it as a gift from God and allow it to come alive and activate it. It takes courage to change things!

Psalm 31:24 Be strong and let your heart take courage, all you who wait for and hope for and expect the Lord!

We must do our part in faith and choose to have the patience to trust in God, who is working behind the scenes for our benefit! He is the God of restoration. Rekindle the hope in your heart. Your life counts! Impossible things that seem absolutely hopeless! Never give up and hold on to the power of hope, activating it with all His might!

Have a hopeful day!

Day 206
HOW'S YOUR SPEECH LATELY?

It is very important to do our part in maintaining peace and harmony via our speech. So, how is your language? The power of words is expansive and amazing; it can build us up and give life or it can tear us down and bring destruction.

Ephesians 4:29 Let no foul or polluting language, nor evil word nor unwholesome or worthless talk (ever) come out of your mouth, but only such (speech) as is good and beneficial to the spiritual progress of others, as is fitting to the need and the occasion, that it may be a blessing and give grace (God's favor) to those who hear it.

Our speech greatly affects us and others.

Ephesians 4:1 Be eager and strive earnestly to guard and keep the harmony and oneness of the Spirit in the binding power of peace.

Pleasant, edifying words always bring peace and build people up. If we have trouble in the way we speak and what we say, pray that God's Spirit will help us day by day to be more like Him.

Luke 1:37 For nothing is impossible with God.

Have a pondering day!

Day 207
PRAISING THE LORD IN ANY SITUATION

We have to be aware and remember that there is a time when God gives to us and there will be a time that He takes away from us. Regardless of which time it is in our lives, we must praise the Lord. Like the story of Job, God gave him a great abundance in family, servants, cattle, etc.. He was the greatest man among all the people of the East. There was also a time that his family, health and possessions were all taken away. Yet, Job still chose to praise God.

Job 1:20-21 At this time, Job got up and tore his robe and shaved his head. Then he fell to the ground in worship and said: "Naked I came from my mother's womb, and naked I will depart. The Lord gave and the Lord has taken away; may the name of the Lord be praised.

What great faith and love Job had for God despite all the distress and turmoil he faced. He knows very well that God is the ultimate source who blesses in his life.

1 Thessalonians 5:16-18 Be joyful always; pray continually; give thanks in all circumstances, for this is God's will for you in Christ Jesus.

When we put God first, blessings always follow.

Have a glorious day!

Day 208
PRECIOUS GIFT OF WISDOM

Have you ever had one of those "Aha" moments when a spark of revelation clicked deep inside you? Let us pray for God's wisdom and revelation as He guides us in handling difficult, questionable matters. Let us be guided by His Spirit and truth to deeply know God, who gives freely as we humbly ask in His name.

Ephesians 1:17-18 I keep asking that the God of our Lord Jesus Christ, the glorious Father, may give you the Spirit of wisdom and revelation, so that you may know Him better. I pray also that the eyes of your heart may be enlightened in order that you may know hope to which he has called you, the riches of his glorious inheritance in the saints.

The value of wisdom is far more precious than gold, silver and rubies!

Proverbs 3:21-23 My son, let them not escape from your sight, but keep sound and godly wisdom and discretion. And they will be life to your inner self, and a gracious ornament to your neck (your outer self). Then you will walk in your way securely and in confident trust, and you shall not dash your foot or stumble.

We receive wisdom, staying in God's word and learning through your life's experiences all that God has taught you. As we continue to pray for God's wisdom, let us have many enlightening moments as we grow to know Him better!

Have an insightful day!

Day 209
THE KEY TO PEACE

How easy it is to lose peace, when unexpected things happen in life that can get you off track! Worries and anxieties can quickly creep up and take over our minds. Put every effort not to allow that to happen! Let us instead immediately fix our mind and heart on God, our everlasting rock!

Isaiah 26:3-4 You will guard him and keep him in perfect and constant peace whose mind is stayed on you, leans on you, and hope confidently in you. So trust in the Lord (commit yourself to Him, lean on Him, Hope confidently in Him) forever; for the Lord God is an everlasting rock (the Rock of Ages).

The main ingredients are to trust, lean, and hope in God. He promises to take care of you. Do not allow the enemy to distract and defeat your mind! Let us not waste our energy on worrying about tomorrow, for it will take care of itself. Let our mind lead us to peace by focusing on God and His wonderful promises to us. The sooner you fix your mind on God, the better off you will be in the direction of peace!

Have a steadfast day!

Day 210
WHEN THINGS GET TOUGH, DON'T GIVE UP

It is entirely too easy to give up when we grow weary and fail to see any immediate results. However, God tells us to never give up and in due time, we shall reap what we've sown.

Galatians 6:9 And let us not lose heart and grow weary and faint in acting nobly and doing right, for in due time and at the appointed season we shall reap, if we do not loosen and relax our courage and faint.

Believers have the mind of Christ, who never complained, grew weary, or gave up. Let us prepare our minds by thinking victoriously in every manner and situations in our lives. Trust in God's timing that all things will work out well for those who love Him and don't lose heart. It will be worth the fight and blessings which will come. The opportunities in which God teaches us patience and endurance stretc.hes and builds our faith in Him. Always remember, when things get tough, don't give up.

Philippians 4:13 I can do all things through Christ who strengthens me.

Have a strong day!

Day 211
EXPRESS AND SPEAK WORDS OF LIFE

Haven't you noticed when we are feeling down and out, a good encouraging word from someone can lift our souls and make us feel better?

Proverbs 12:25   Anxiety in a man's heart weighs it down, but an encouraging word makes it glad.

Encouraging words are like living water. God wants us to express and speak words of life to others.

Proverbs 18:4   The words of a (discreet and wise) man's mouth are like deep waters, and the fountain of skillful and godly Wisdom is like a gushing stream (sparkling, fresh, pure, and life-giving).

Let us use the power of our tongues to bring life to ourselves and others. Pleasant words can bring healing to your mind and body.

Proverbs 16:24   Pleasant words are as a honey-comb, sweet to the mind and healing to the body.

We have the power to give good medicine to others. Let us be encouraged to use our words wisely.

Have a thought provoking day!

Day 212
TESTS ARE FOR OUR OWN GOOD

Doesn't the word "test" just make you cringe? It especially does so if you're not ready for it. But when you've been studying and getting ready any way possible, you may say "Bring it on!" Only God knows when it is time or when we're ready to take a test.

Psalm 7:9 Oh, let the wickedness of the wicked come to an end, but establish the (uncompromisingly) righteous (those upright and in harmony with you); for you, Who try the hearts and emotions and thinking powers, are a righteous God.

God gives us tests for our own good, to see the quality of our character. Only through the pressures of life does our true character come out! He wants to build up our stability, to make us strong and steadfast in Him, so we can walk in the fruit of the Holy Spirit regardless of how we *feel*. When you feel that your emotions and how you think are out of control, take a deep breath and say to yourself, "I'm going to trust God and learn to control myself." We learn and grow through the challenges of our tests. Remember, only God knows how much you can handle! Ask God to give you the grace to pass all your tests!

Have a triumphant day!

Day 213
FILL UP WITH GOD

God has intentionally placed a void in our hearts only He can fill because He wants a relationship with us. People try to fill their voids with all kinds of things, possessions, relationships, job statuses, and addictions. There is nothing that can fill your void to the fullest than Jesus.

John 10:10 I came that they may have and enjoy life, and have it in abundance (to the full, till it overflows).

There is also nothing that can separate you from the love of God.

Romans 8:38-39 For I am convinced that neither death nor life, neither angels nor demons, neither the present nor the future, nor any powers, neither height nor depth, nor anything else in all creation, will be able to separate us from the love of God that is in Christ Jesus our Lord.

Once we accept God into our heart and lives, allow Him to fill you up with His great love and know that He will never leave you nor forsake you in any way. That is His promise to you so take comfort in that. God knows you inside and out and He knows your every need.

Jeremiah 1:5 Before I formed you in the womb I knew you, before you were born I set you apart; I appointed you as a prophet to the nations.

Always trust in God's loving grace for you and accept His overflowing love and His abundant life within you.

Have a magnificent day!

Day 214
A PERFECT EXAMPLE OF OBEDIENCE

How far will you go in obedience? If someone you love asked you to do something far above your reach and capabilities, will you attempt to go the extra mile for them? Jesus went far above His obedience to God by dying on the cross *for us.*

Philippians 2:8 And after He had appeared in human form, He abased and humbled Himself (still further) and carried his obedience to the extreme of death, even the death of the cross!

Just imagine if Jesus chose not to obey God by His death on the cross because He didn't *feel like it.* Destruction would have come to all of us! Praise God that He saved us from our sins. Jesus set the perfect example for obedience; let us choose to raise the bar of obedience in our lives by obeying God's word. His Word is perfect in truth, hope and righteousness. It is important to make decisions not based on how you feel, but rather to do what is right and good in submission and obedience to God! Blessings always follow after obedience.

Have a humbling day!

Day 215
STOP COMPLAINING AND COME TO YOUR SENSES

Daily complaints and bad attitudes get us nowhere. They only set us up for downfall and miseries, are a complete waste of time and energy, and are not good for our health.

Numbers 14:2-3 All the Israelites grumbled against Moses and Aaron, and the whole assembly said to them, "If only we had died in Egypt! Or in this desert! Why is the Lord bringing us to this land only to let us fall by the sword? Our wives and children will be taken as plunder. Wouldn't it be better for us to go back to Egypt?"

It's too bad that the Israelites didn't trust in God enough to see the hope in His promises of bringing them into the Promise Land. He wanted nothing but good things for them and their future but they got sick and tired of being out in the wilderness and even wanted to go back to Egypt, where they were kept in bondage. They were not in their right minds. Whatever kinds of past addictions, bad habits, or bondage you were once in and delivered out of, praise God for it and move forward without complaining, yearning, or whining. Instead, trust in God's promises for your life of hope and victories.

Have a sensible day!

Day 216
YOU DON'T WANT TO MISS OUT

There is one thing in life that I hope we won't want to regret, and that is to miss out on all of God's goodness and blessings in our lives.

Psalm 27:13   (What, what would have become of me) had I not believed that I would see the Lord's goodness in the land of the living!

Experiencing the good life in God is to always be in His presence!

Psalm 27:4   One thing have I asked of the Lord, that will I seek, inquire for, and require; that I may dwell in the house of the Lord all the days of my life, to behold and gaze upon the beauty of the Lord and to meditate, consider, and inquire in His temple.

Keep on seeking God, get to know Him intimately, to build a wonderful relationship with Him. Nothing in life can fill any kind of void or emptiness inside of us, but only God can and will to complete fulfillment! It is vital that we seek Him and dwell in His presence!

John 10:10 (I came that they may have and enjoy life, and have it in abundance (to the full, till it overflows).

Let us not be mislead to listen to the lies of the world that position, power, possessions, etc., will meet your every need! Only God completely fills you up with living water continuing to overflow. Let us seek our true God and not miss out.

Have a wonderful day!

Day 217
GOD'S SPIRIT SPEAKING FOR YOU

Is there a time when you feel inadequate on what to say? Let us not look too much from within our own capabilities, but rather put our trust and faith in God who is the source and maker of our mouths.

Exodus 3:12 Now go; I will help you speak and will teach you what to say.

Moses felt inadequate in his speaking abilities and his ability to the Israelites out of Egypt. God told him not to worry because He would help him on what to say at the given time. Yielding our spirit to God, He will help you say what needs to be said. You will be truly amazed what comes out of your mouths, because you know it wasn't you, but God's Spirit speaking for you. We should not worry or fear when we have to talk to that certain someone, a spouse, co worker, friend, or parent. Pray and allow God to speak through you.

Have a mind blowing day!

Day 218
HOPE AND EXPECT SOMETHING GOOD

There seems to be a pattern when recalling your past goodness, therefore putting great hope and expectations for your future. We can easily forget God's faithfulness, mercy, loving-kindness, and his tender compassion for us.

Lamentations 3:21-23 But this I recall and therefore have I hope and expectation: It is because of the Lord's mercy and loving-kindness that we are not consumed, because His (tender) compassions fail not.. They are new every morning; great and abundant is Your stability and faithfulness.

Verse 25: The Lord is good to those who wait hopefully and expectantly for Him, to those who seek Him.

Let us be in the attitude of waiting patiently and seeking earnestly for God to do His mighty work. Where do you put your focus when in tough times? Let us be encouraged to focus on God's goodness to us. His mercies and kindness are new every single morning and beyond limitless! Let us hope and expect something truly *good*! It'll help you to stay alive in your heart and spirit, and to be positive.

Have an expectant day!

Day 219
A PERMANENT PERSONAL RELATIONSHIP
WITH GOD

The reason God created us in this world is to have a relationship with Him. Nothing delights and pleases Him more than for us, in our own free will and choice, to know God and to develop an everlasting relationship with Him. He did not create us to be robots automatically set to love Him. No, He gave us a free will.

Jeremiah 32:38-41 They will be my people , and I will be their God. I will give them singleness of heart and action, so that they will always fear me for their own good and the good of their children after them. I will make an everlasting covenant with them: I will never stop doing good to them, and I will inspire them to fear me, so that they will never turn away from me. I will rejoice in doing them good and will assuredly plant them in this land with all my heart and soul.

See the incredible relationship we can have with our Almighty God? What a privilege! He puts fear into us, so that we may continue on our right path with Him. He wants nothing but good for us and our children. Keeping our focus on Him with a single heart and action is where we want to be. Let us be encouraged to develop an intimate, permanent, personal relationship with God.

Have a beautiful day!

Day 220
OUR MYSTERIOUS, AWESOME GOD

There may be some people you think that you have all figured out, and you are able to pinpoint what their next plans and behaviors may be.

Romans 11:33-34 Oh, the depth of the riches and wisdom and knowledge of God! How unfathomable are His judgments (his decisions)! And how untraceable (mysterious, undiscoverable) are His ways (His methods, His paths)! For who has the mind of the Lord and who has understood His thoughts, or who has (ever) been His counselor?

God works in mysterious ways! He is the only one we cannot figure out! Do not even try to figure Him out. Just get to know Him, have faith and believe in Him, and trust him completely. God is the ultimate being. There is no one higher or above Him. His plans and ways really are smarter and better than ours! Go to Him for your every need and your heart's desire. He loves you so, and is looking out for your best interests. He needs and wants our faith in Him!

Have an awe-struck day!

Day 221
TIRED OF BEING CONTROLLED BY YOUR SINFUL NATURE?

Have you come to a place in your life where you are tired of being controlled by your sinful nature? Yield to God's Spirit. As a child of God, we have His Spirit living inside of us. Therefore, let us yield to and allow God's Spirit to control us in everything good and pleasing to God.

Romans 8:8-10 Those controlled by the sinful nature cannot please God. You, however, are controlled not by the sinful nature but by the Spirit, if the Spirit of God lives in you. And if anyone does not have the Spirit of Christ, he does not belong to Christ. But if Christ is in you, your body is dead because of sin, yet your Spirit is alive because of righteousness.

It's a guarantee that as we yield to the Spirit, we put to death our sinful nature and become a new creation in Christ and live a life of freedom and victory. Our main goal should be to please God in everything. As we take our steps toward leaning on God's Spirit every day, you'll be wonderfully surprised that, little by little, your bad habits dissipate.

Have a liberating day!

Day 222
YOUR CHOICE OF DISSATISFACTION OR CONTENTMENT

Why does it seem to appear that the grass is always greener on the other side? When we see and hear of other people's greater fortunes, materials, talents, families, etc., it can leave us with great discontent! God tells us not to covet other people's things.

Exodus 20:17   You shall not covet your neighbor's house, your neighbor's wife, or his manservant, or his maidservant, or his ox, or his donkey, or anything that is your neighbor's.

It is very important to learn to be content with what God has given to you! Don't bother with other people's things, but instead, look to the wonderful blessings God has bestowed upon you and be grateful. We cannot judge others from the outside; who knows their story of how they got their "stuff" in life! Everyone has their own story! Being discontent only brings dissatisfaction, envy, jealousy, and all the ugly feelings inside. Who wants to live in that state of mind?

Let us learn to be content with our own uniqueness and all of God's gifts that bring joy, peace, and fulfillment to us. It's up to you to choose your mindset! God have given to us an abundant life to enjoy and let us relish in it!

Have a happy day!

Day 223
IT REALLY CAN BE WORSE

Have you ever thought to yourself that things cannot be any worse? But, it really can be worse! We have to learn to be content in whatever state that we are in!

Philippians 4:11 Not that I am implying that I was in any personal want, for I have learned how to be content (satisfied to the point where I am not disturbed or disquieted) in whatever state I am.

There may be a reason we are in our present condition. Maybe it's to teach us humility, appreciation, patience, or just looking to God for our every need. Let us trust Him for everything.

Psalm 16:7 I will bless the Lord, Who has given me counsel; Yes, my heart instructs me in the night seasons.

Proverbs 14:30 A calm and undisturbed mind and heart are life and health of the body, but envy, jealousy, and wrath are like rottenness of the bones.

Let us look to God for His wonderful teachings, for a calm mind and heart is health to the body! If we are always in the want and not satisfied, we are only hurting ourselves.

Philippians 4:19 And my God will liberally supply (fill to the full) your every need according to His riches in glory in Christ Jesus.

God knows exactly what we need. Trust in Him no matter what and learn to be content!

Have a fulfilled day!

Day 224
NURTURING HEALTHY RELATIONSHIPS

How do we nurture healthy relationships? We all desire good, strong, healthy relationships, but dealing with people can be very challenging at times.

1 Peter 3:9-11 Do not repay evil with evil or insult with insult, but with blessing, because to this you were called so that you may inherit blessing. For, whoever would love life and see good days must keep his tongue from evil and his lips from deceitful speech. He must turn from evil and do good; he must seek peace and pursue it.

When we get hurt or insulted, we automatically want to attack back but God tells us to resist ourselves and hold our tongues and instead, bless and pray for them. If we want to see good days ahead in peace, we must put love before everything.

1 Corinthians 13:4-6 Love is patient, love is kind. It does not envy, it does not boast, it is not proud. It is not rude, it is not self-seeking, it is not easily angered, it keeps no record of wrongs. Love does not delight in evil, but rejoices with the truth.

Everything about God is love. Let us pray for strength and wisdom and remember God in all your relationships. Love is the key to peace, joy, and happiness.

Have a healthy, peaceful day!

Day 225
A FORK IN THE ROAD

Have you wondered what kind of decisions to make and are not quite sure if they are good and right? We may go by our own precepts and think they are right.

John 7:17 If any man desires to do His will (God's pleasure), he will know (have the needed illumination to recognize, and can tell for himself) whether the teaching is from God or whether I am speaking from Myself and of My own accord and on My own authority.

Our main goal and purpose should be to honor and glorify God! The key is to fear and worship Him.

Psalm 25:14   The secret (of the sweet, satisfying companionship) of the Lord have they who fear (revere and worship) Him, and He will show them His covenant and reveal to them its (deep inner) meaning.

Only when we try to do the things we want to do, it can lead us toward frustrations, uneasiness, and doubts. Let us surrender and trust in God's plans, and the ways that He has planned out for our lives. You will surely then be at ease!

Have a great day!

Day 226
KINDNESS IS ATTRACTIVE

There must be a reason why the saying goes "Kill them with kindness." Kindness makes us look attractive inside and out! There is great power in being kind and gracious. A beautiful person has the ability to look less attractive by his or her bitterness, anger, quarreling and unforgiving ways.

Ephesians 4:31-32 Get rid of all bitterness, rage and anger, brawling and slander, along with every form of malice. Be kind and compassionate to one another, forgiving each other, just as in Christ God forgave you.

The perfect example of Christ's forgiveness is when He was hanging on the cross after being beat, ridiculed, pierced with nails and thorns, offended, etc., but yet He prayed to God saying, "Forgive them, for they do not know what they are doing." He knew that we are all broken people and do not know any better! That is why He died for us to save us from our sins.

Ephesians 5:1-2 Be imitators of God, therefore, as dearly loved children and live a life of love, just as Christ loved us and gave Himself up for us as a fragrant offering and sacrifice to God.

Let us pray that our beauty may shine brightly by letting go of all the ugliness, bitterness, resentment, bad temper, evil speaking, and all other unforgiving things! We will not only be attractive in our eyes and the eyes of others, but in God's eyes where it matters and counts. The eyes, heart and spirit of a kind and loving person is a true winner!

Have an attracting day!

Day 227
WIN THE FAVOR OF GOD, NOT MEN

Ok, sometimes we have to say to ourselves, "Enough is enough!" It is enough of trying to please others all the time. God says that we cannot be pleasers of both men and God.

Galatians 1:10 Now am I trying to win the favor of men, or of God? Do I seek to please men? If I were still seeking popularity with men, I should not be a bond servant of Christ.

If we were to keep or focus on pleasing God, peace and joy enters. As we know, we can never satisfy everyone all the time, which leaves us with no satisfaction in always trying to chase the rainbow! We must learn to use discernment and practice saying "No" to people, and to be okay with some of them not liking what you are doing. Our rewards always come from the motivation of ultimately pleasing God in every way! Don't allow people to get you off balance. It is our responsibility to keep ourselves in check for our peace and health. Think twice before you say "yes" to everyone and everything.

Have a favorable day!

Day 228
YOUR PURPOSE IN YOUR GENERATION

Life is fleeting and it passes by so rapidly. Think about your significance here on earth. We are urged not to waste our lives. Let us take a look at the big picture God has planned out for us in our lives as we make significant differences in the lives of others: your family, friends, coworkers and community. Life is all about relationships and the kind of impact we leave on them.

Acts 13:36 For David, after he had served God's will and purpose and counsel in his own generation, fell asleep (in death).

King David was a man after God's own heart. Let him be our example on how to live the life God intends for us, seeking God's heart. Our goal, as believers, should be to end our lives by saying, "I have fought the good fight of faith, righteousness and God's glory." When we are focused on God and doing His will in everything that we do, we can do no wrong. We are living the blessed and abundant life in Him. We are put here at this time, in this generation, for a purpose. Be all that you can be for God's glory.

Have a meaningful day!

Day 229
LIVE INTENTIONALLY

Everyone has a unique time limit that God has graciously given to them, living here on earth. While we are alive today, we should have the attitude of living passionately, purposefully, and gratefully!

Psalm 90:12 So teach us to number our days, that we may get us a heart of wisdom.

How sad it is to hear when people choose to live a foolish, self-centered life and constantly make bad choices. We have only one life to live. Let's make it count for something good in God's kingdom! If we were to hear that we had a month to live, I'm sure our attitude would become more intentional! We would not waste a moment of regret to tell others how much we love and appreciate them, and would have a desire to leave a wonderful legacy. What we choose to do with our time, efforts and energies are all up to us. If we have nothing but regrets in life, then it is never too late to make things good and right! Let us truly enjoy and appreciate all of God's goodness in our lives! The wonderful people around us, good circumstances, health, jobs, living conditions, etc.; they are not an accident! We are truly blessed! Let us praise God each and every day, and *live*. Live intentionally, making our life count, living in wisdom!

Have a lively day!

Day 230
IT'S SURELY A GOOD LIFE

I'm sure we are all familiar with the Christmas movie *It's a Wonderful Life* featuring Jimmy Stewart. After endless problems and challenging situations in his life, one day he came to the end of his rope and decided to kill himself. He wished he had never been born. An angel appeared and showed him how life would have been if he had never existed. He came to his senses after seeing all the lives of people he had touched by helping them in their right path for their lives. He then valued his family, friends, community and his existence! We can all get caught up in life's many circumstances, but God wants us to know and realize that we surely have a good life in Him!

Ephesians 2:10 For we are God's (own) handiwork (His workmanship), recreated in Christ Jesus, (born anew) that we may do those good works which God predestined (planned beforehand) for us (taking paths which He prepared ahead of time), that we should walk in them (living the good life which He prearranged and made ready for us to live).

Let us value, appreciate, enjoy and live this good life that God has prepared for us! Even though we may have made mistakes in our past, let us trust in His ways and stay on our right path for Him! Our life matters and counts a great deal to God and to others. Instead of complaining, let us cultivate a grateful heart! Now, enjoy your life to the fullest. God deserves all praise and glory!

Have a wonderful day!

Day 231
THE JOY OF THE LORD IS OUR STRENGTH

God desires for us to praise Him morning, noon and night.

Psalm 147:1 How good to sing praises to our God! How delightful and how fitting.

Giving God praise that He so deserves can change us and our environment.

1 Thessalonians 5:18 In everything give thanks; for this is the will of God in Christ Jesus for you.

Praise God by singing and meditating on Him day and night. It lifts us up and reminds us on how good and magnificent God is. A wonderful part of building our relationship with God is to fellowship with Him by giving Him praise.

Psalm 118:24 This is the day which the Lord has brought about; we will rejoice and be glad in it.

Let us choose to be happy in and through Christ, for the joy of the Lord is our strength.

Have an uplifting day!

Day 232
THE REASON GOD HATES PRIDE

Can you imagine one of the things that God hates? It is pride! He knows that it eventually leads us towards destruction.

Proverbs 16:18 Pride goes before destruction, and a haughty spirit before a fall.

Jesus represented ultimate humility, even up to His death on the cross.

Proverbs 29:23 A man's pride will bring him low, but he who is of a humble spirit will obtain honor.

What a contrast! Do you want destruction or honor in your life? It all starts with reverently fearing God.

Proverbs 15:33 The reverent and worshipful fear of the Lord brings instruction in wisdom, and humility comes before honor.

Pray for wisdom.

Proverbs 4:8 Prize Wisdom highly and exalt her, and she will exalt and promote you; she will bring you to honor when you embrace her.

Let us pray that our pride will not get in the way of first fearing God, which leads us to humility and then to great honor. Let us walk humbly before our God in sweet surrender.

Have a softening day!

Day 233
ENOUGH EXCUSES

Why is it that we don't like to take responsibility in certain matters? Even little children like to point the finger at someone else and say "It's all your fault and *you* made me do this!" It all started with Adam and Eve.

Genesis 3:11-13 And he said, "Who told you that you were naked? Have you eaten of the tree of which I commanded you that you should not eat?" And the man said, "The woman whom you gave to be with me- she gave me (fruit) from the tree, and I ate it." And the Lord God said to the woman, "What is this you have done?" And the woman said, "The serpent beguiled (cheated, outwitted, and deceived) me, and I ate it."

We must take responsibility of our own actions. It is way too easy to keep blaming other people, mishaps in life, or unfair situations! The enemy wants to continue to deceive us into thinking we are always a victim of some sort. Do not believe these lies. If we choose to continue to listen to his lies, then we reap the consequences of our actions.

Genesis 3:17 And to Adam He said, "Because you have listened and given heed to the voice of your wife and have eaten of the tree of which I commanded you, saying, 'You shall not eat of it,' the ground is under a curse because of you; in sorrow and toil shall you eat of it all the days of your life.

Let's be encouraged to take responsibility in our choices and actions and to stop blaming others! Then we can go on living in God's peace and the richness of life given to us.

Have a responsible day!

Day 234
DON'T GIVE UP! BLESSINGS ARE SOON TO FOLLOW

How easy it is to give up what is good and right when we are emotionally, physically or spiritually tired and weary. God tells us to keep up the fight so that we do not miss out on our blessings!

Galatians 6:9 And let us not lose heart and grow weary and faint in acting nobly and doing right, for in due time and at the appointed season we shall reap, if we do not loosen and relax our courage and faint.

God tells us to be the best people we can be. He commands us to be a great parent, wonderful spouse, an excellent worker, a good friend, a child of God, etc.. Only God knows our limitations and He sees the best in us. Don't allow yourself to lose heart and grow weary. Don't even think about throwing in the towel. Never quit because wonderful blessings are just around the corner. We shall reap what we've sown. God rewards you for doing what's right so don't be surprised when blessings come from all your good efforts.

Have a sustaining day!

Day 235
FIRST CALL UPON GOD, IN TIMES OF NEED

Who do you usually call upon during your time of need, or do you just try to rely upon yourself to fix the problem? God tells us to call upon Him first and foremost!

Psalm 91:14-15 Because he has set his love upon Me, therefore will I deliver him; I will set him on high, because he knows and understands my name (has a personal knowledge of My mercy, love, and kindness-trusts and relies on Me, knowing I will never forsake him, no never). He shall call upon Me, and I will answer him; I will be with him in trouble, I will deliver him and honor him.

Having a personal relationship with God is of the utmost necessity and privilege in our life. Getting to know God's character and loving Him with your whole heart is very important. Go to God first before other people or trying to help yourself. His ways are the best ways and He knows your troubles, and promises to help deliver you. Trust in Him for your every need. The sooner you go to Him, the greater the outcome will be!

Have an inviting day!

Day 236
SELF DOUBT BE GONE! GET READY TO BE MARVELED

Sometimes we may feel inadequate to do certain things, and we constantly make excuses! Doubts seem to always be on our minds. God wants us to rise up in faith and believe that He can use us for anything and everything He desires for us!

Exodus 4: 10-12 And Moses said to the Lord, O Lord, I am not eloquent or a man of words, neither before nor since You have spoken to Your servant; for I am slow of speech and have a heavy and awkward tongue. And the Lord said to Him, Who has made man's mouth? Or who makes the dumb, or the deaf, or the seeing, or the blind? Is it not I, the Lord? Now therefore go, and I will be with your mouth and will teach you what you shall say.

The key here is to have full confidence in God. Regardless of anything you lack in yourself, God can make a way for you to succeed! Start now to get rid of self doubt and instead let confidence in Christ rule in you. When you allow God to intervene in your situations, get ready to be marveled!

Have a guaranteed day!

Day 237
ENJOY WHERE YOU ARE AT

How challenging it can be to enjoy our positions in life when we are unhappy and struggling. We may think to ourselves, "How can I enjoy where I'm at when I'm so busy with my job, raising kids, keeping up with my schedule, doing house chores, etc..?" God tells us to enjoy every moment of our lives because we are truly blessed. Instead of harboring negativity, let us change our attitudes and perspectives on all the people and things God has given to us in praise and thanks to Him.

1 Thessalonians 5:16-18   Rejoice always, pray continually, give thanks in all circumstances; for this is God's will for you in Jesus Christ.

God freely gives to us, and at any moment, it can be taken away. Our situations really can be worse, so be grateful for all the things we have! Let us learn to appreciate and enjoy every moment of our lives with a thankful heart and always remember to stop and smell the flowers. It all begins with our choice of attitude. Let us be encouraged to be filled with God's Spirit and see God in and through everything.

Have a blessed day!

Day 238
DO NOT BE ANXIOUS

Anxiety can kick in when we're not too sure about our plans in our lives. For example, we may be ambivalent on how to raise our children, the next project, or job. God tells us not to worry because His presence will always be with us to give us the assurance and rest in Him.

Exodus 33:14 And the Lord said, My presence shall go with you, and I will give you rest.

Moses was worried and concerned about how to lead the Israelites out of Egypt. He had no idea how to go about executing the plan but God assured Him that His presence would always be with Him. God would lead and guide him in every manner. To be in God's presence is to live in comfort and peace. When we feel worried and anxious about certain things, let us focus on God and He will give you rest for your souls. When we take our eyes off of God and rely on our own strength, anxiety arises. Let us be encouraged to take one day at a time and march through our plans with God's presence.

Have an assured day!

Day 239
THE IMPORTANCE OF PATIENCE

Wouldn't it be nice if we all had an automatic quality of patience? Can you just imagine how our mindset and lifestyle would be like? We would definitely have no frustrations and anxieties taking place from within. Patience is a learned skill! God tells us to have patience.

James 5:7-8 So be patient, brethren, (as you wait) till the coming of the Lord. See how the farmer waits expectantly for the precious harvest from the land. (See how) he keeps up his patient over it until it receives the early and late rains. So you also must be patient. Establish your hearts (strengthen and confirm them in the final certainty), for the coming of the Lord is very near.

The very best is worth the wait! When we give into our impatient ways, we can miss out on the beautiful opportunities and blessings that are in stored for us. Let us be encouraged to wait on God with a good attitude, trusting that he orchestrates everything to the minute detail and timing in our lives! Let's not go ahead with our own plans and miss out on His harvest of abundant blessings! Patience can get you far and give you the peace we long for.

Have a wonderful day!

Day 240
ACCEPT ONE ANOTHER

How challenging can it be to welcome and accept one another? Especially when our personalities clash and we have no similarities. We may talk, dress or act differently from each other, and the list goes on and on. God tells us to accept one another no matter what!

Romans 15:7 Welcome and receive (to your hearts) one another, then, even as Christ has welcomed and received you, for the glory of God.

We should do everything for the glory of God and make it a priority to please Him. Christ gave us the perfect example by receiving us for God's glory. We must remember to put ourselves aside and realize it's not about "me, myself, and I", but about what God asks of us, which is to love and accept one another in Christ! Our purpose is to be unified, praising and glorifying God together. Being kind and gracious is always a winner!

Have an accepting day!

Day 241
HANDLING DIFFICULTIES AND HARDSHIPS

Difficulties and hardships are inevitable. However, how we deal with misfortune varies but God wants us to go to Him in every way.

Psalm 57:1-3 Have mercy on me, O God, have mercy on me, for in my soul takes refuge. I will take refuge in the shadow of your wings until the disaster has passed. I cry out to God Most High, to God, who fulfills His purpose for me. He sends from heaven and saves me, rebuking those who hotly pursue me: God sends is love and his faithfulness.

Go to God as our protector. Know that the storms will pass. In the meantime, take refuge in the shadow of God's almighty wings knowing confidently that He will work on our behalf. He has a purpose for every matter and by our right attitude and faith, when it is completed, our character builds in Him. He will protect us from our enemies with His mercy, loving kindness, His truth and faithfulness. Let us be encouraged to give all our weight and burdens to God and rest in the shadow of His wings. Hold onto His promises for you.

Have a peaceful day!

Day 242
GET READY TO BE ASTONISHED

When we make appointments, we wait for that certain date and time for the appointment to follow through. Do not be discouraged during the wait for God has an appointed time and event for matters in our lives. He is never early or late with His schedule.

Habakkuk 1:2 O Lord, how long shall I cry for help and You will not hear? Or cry out to You of violence and You will not save?

All your prayers and requests are not in vain. God surely does hear you.

Habakkuk 1:5 Look around you (you, Habakkuk, replied the Lord) among the nations and see! And be astonished! Astounded! For I am putting into effect a work in your days that you would not believe it if it were told you.

Stay in faith for something wonderful is going to happen.

Habakkuk 2:3 For the vision is yet for an appointed time and it hastens to the end (fulfillment); it will not deceive or disappoint. Though it tarry, wait (earnestly) for it, because it will surely come; it will not be behindhand on its appointed day.

Never give up hope amidst trials and tribulations. God has a good plan for us and is working behind the scenes in our lives. He keeps His appointments on all incredible blessings.

Have a faith-filled day!

Day 243
KEEP IT SIMPLE

Notice when we have more goods or riches, our lives can get more complicated and stressful. When we keep our lives simple, we can sleep better!

Ecclesiastes 5:11-13 When goods increase, they who eat them increase also. And what gain is there to their owner except to see them with his eyes? The sleep of a laboring man is sweet, whether he eats little or much, but the fullness of the rich will not let him sleep. There is a serious and severe evil which I have seen under the sun; riches were kept by their owner to his hurt.

We are only hurting ourselves when we focus and concentrate on making more money, gaining more goods, or having the desire to keep on accumulating all the "stuff" in this world. It can only lead to stress and headaches! Be careful not to allow that to happen, and to not allow them to *own you*! Living within your means and keeping your lives as simple as possible is where you want to be. In peace and contentment and fulfilled joy!

Have a peaceful day!

Day 244
REALLY KNOW HOW MUCH GOD LOVES YOU

Sometimes we may not like to see how we truly are as people. God knows very well (because he created us) that we are all broken people and are prisoners of this world. We are held captive by sins such as addictions, pride, lust, jealousy, greed, bitterness, etc.. By wanting to set us free from our sins, God sent His Son Jesus Christ to die on the cross to save us from ourselves! Know how much God really loves you.

Luke 4:18-19 The Spirit of the Lord (is) upon Me, because He has anointed Me to preach the good news (the gospel) to the poor; He has sent Me to announce release to the captives and recovery of sight to the blind, to send forth as delivered those who are oppressed (who are downtrodden, bruised, crushed, and broken down by calamity).

Jesus sets the prisoner free! Believe today that freedom in Christ is possible and real!

1 Peter 1-18-19 For you know that it was not with perishable things such as silver or gold that you were redeemed from the empty way of life handed down to your forefathers, but with the precious blood of Christ, a lamb without blemish or defect...Through Him you believe in God, Who raised Him from the dead and glorified Him, and so your faith and hope are in God.

What an ultimate sacrifice of Jesus dying on the cross for us! God loves you and wants the best for you and has a perfect plan for your life! Praise God!

Have an endearing day!

Day 245
WHO ARE WE TO JUDGE?

One thing that seems to be an automatic response when we see and hear about others is to judge. Who are we to judge? We do not truly know the heart and story of every person, and they do not know ours. Only God does, and He is the great judge.

Romans 2:1 You, therefore have no excuse, you who pass judgment on someone else, for at whatever point you judge the other, you are condemning yourself, because you who pass judgment do the same things.

Maybe people judge because it makes them feel better and superior than others. God created and made us all as equals in His own image. He knows very well that we are all imperfect and broken in one way or another. God's kindness should lead us towards repentance.

Romans 2:4 Or are you (so blind as to) trifle with and presume upon and despise and underestimate the wealth of His kindness and forbearance and long suffering patience? Are you unmindful or actually ignorant (of the fact) that God's kindness is intended to lead you to repent (to change your mind and inner man to accept God's will)?

Thank goodness for the grace, love and mercy of God whose kindness leads us to repent. How many times have we said to another that we are sorry for misjudging them? Let us be encouraged not to judge and instead, leave the judging to God.

Have a neutral day!

Day 246
REASONS FOR UPLIFTED FACES

As believers, there is a genuine reason for our uplifted faces.

Psalm 89:15-17 Blessed are the people who know the joyful sound (who understand and appreciate the spiritual blessings symbolized by the feasts); they walk, O Lord, in the light and favor of your countenance! In your name they rejoice all the day, and in Your righteousness they are exalted. For You are the glory of their strength (their proud adornment), and by Your favor our horn is exalted and we walk with uplifted faces!

What a privilege it is to walk with uplifted faces knowing we are God's children and that He is the source of our strength! We know, in our weakness, God is strong and mighty. Let us walk tall with confidence and wear proudly the adornment of God's strength. With God on our side, we can conquer anything and victory is ours.

Have a smiling day!

Day 247
A NEW LIFE IN CHRIST

Do you ever wish that you can start over again in your life with a clean slate? God tells us that we can have a new life in Christ!

2 Corinthians 5:17 Therefore, if anyone is in Christ, he is a new creation; the old has gone, the new has come!

By accepting Jesus as our Savior, we have hope in our hearts being born anew.

1 Peter 1:3-4 Praise be to the God and Father of our Lord Jesus Christ! In His great mercy He has given us a new birth into a living hope through the resurrection of Jesus Christ from the dead, and into an inheritance that can never perish, spoil or fade-kept in Heaven for you.

We have salvation and a brand new life in Christ! The Holy Spirit dwells inside of us, helping us along with our new life in Him. We get to see things from God's perspective and enjoy all of life's goodness that He offers to us! Praise God that there is a way to get rid of the old and come into the new. You will not be in any regret going into the new, because that is where true blessings and a fulfilled life is found.

Have a beautiful day!

Day 248
THE CRUCIAL MOMENT THAT CHANGED EVERYTHING

There is a time when one moment has changed everything. Jesus paid the sin debt of the whole world in *one moment*!

1 Peter 2:24 He personally bore our sins in His (own) body on the tree (as on an altar and offered Himself on it), that we might die (cease to exist) to sin and live to righteousness. By His wounds you have been healed.

All we have to do is pray and ask for forgiveness of our sins and repent.

Romans 5:17 For if, by the trespass of the one man, death reigned through that one man, how much more will those who receive God's abundant provision of grace and of the gift of righteousness reign in life through the one man, Jesus Christ.

Jesus is the one man that took the one moment of sacrificing Himself to die on the cross for our sins.

Romans 14:17 For the kingdom of God is not a matter of eating and drinking, but of righteousness, peace and joy in the Holy Spirit.

The kingdom of God resides within us along with having God's power and His spirit alive and well, activating full force in our lives! Let us believe and receive this one moment that changed everything for us to have new life in Him!

Have an accepting day!

Day 249
WHOSE APPLAUSE DO YOU SEEK?

For us believers, being in a right relationship with God causes His Spirit to change our hearts toward Him in every way. God wants us not only to obey His law, but also to seek His praise, not the praise of others, in everything that we do. Whose applause do you seek? We want the recognition for doing a job well done, being a good parent, displaying our skills and talents, etc.. Our true desire should be for acclimation from God alone, for His applause. That should be our sole motivation.

Romans 2:29 No, a true Jew is one whose heart is right with God. A true circumcision is not merely obeying the letter of the law; rather, it is a change of the heart produced by God's Spirit. And a person with a changed heart seeks praise from God, not from people.

The rewards and blessings are eternal, everlasting and bountiful with God's approval, compared to the temporal unstable approval of men. Let us think twice about our true motivation for all our works and efforts, seek the everlasting blessings from God, and win His approval.

Have a right focused day!

Day 250
BECAUSE HE LIVES, I CAN FACE TOMORROW

What greater hope and joy is there, than Jesus' resurrection in our lives! The song says "Because He lives, I can face tomorrow, because He lives, all fear is gone. Because I know, He holds the future, and life is worth the living, just because He lives!"

1 Peter1:21 Through Him you believe in God, Who raised Him up from the dead and gave Him honor and glory, so that your faith and hope are (centered and rest) in God.

It's all about Jesus! He did it all for us! He paid our sins on the cross to save and forgive us. Jesus is the bridge to His blessings and internal happiness.

John 10:10 I came that they may have and enjoy life, and have it in abundance (to the full, till it overflows).

Let us live in God's outpouring love and in His wonderful grace, facing all the "tomorrows," because He lives! We are everything we are, because God loves us! Praise God!

Have a magnificent day!

Day 251
NO MORE DOUBTING

Are you the kind of person that needs some proof when hearing or dealing with certain matters? Thomas was that type of person. Even after Jesus rose from the dead, he needed to see some proof that Jesus was alive once again.

John 20:24-29 Now Thomas, one of the Twelve, was not with the disciples when Jesus came. So the other disciples told him, "We have seen the Lord!" But he said to them, "Unless I see the nail marks in His hands and put my finger where the nails were, and put my hand into His side, I will not believe it." A week later his disciples were in the house again, and Thomas was with them. Though the doors were locked, Jesus came and stood among them and said, "Peace be with you!" Then He said to Thomas, "Put your finger here; see my hands. Reach out your hand and put it into my side. Stop doubting and believe." Thomas said to him, "My Lord and my God!" Then Jesus told him, "Because you have seen me, you have believed; Blessed are those who have not seen and yet have believed."

Let us believe and continue to grow stronger in our faith to God; He definitely keeps his promises to us! Doubt leads to disobedience! Remember past events of wavering doubts and how God was there to pull you through, and out of them. Let us muster up our faith and simply have a childlike faith, truly believing all the goodness of God in our lives.

Have an unwavering day!

Day 252
SIN SEPARATES

If we wonder why God is not hearing or answering our prayers, or feel distant from Him, it could be due to a willing and deliberate sin in our lives that has taken a hold of us, which separates us from God.

Isaiah 59:1-2 Behold, The Lord's hand is not shortened at all, that it cannot save, nor His ear dull with deafness, that it cannot hear. But your iniquities have made a separation between you and your God, and your sins have hidden His face from you, so that He will not hear.

Once we ask for forgiveness of our sins and repent, it freely opens up a channel with God and we can build intimacy with Him. Let us pray that the Holy Spirit may help to lead and guide you with courage and desire towards the right direction, to have a clear conscience and to be set in freedom with Christ. Having a clear conscience that is pure and right before God enables us to live the blessed and abundant life, growing in our journey of faith in Him.

What a beautiful exchange of freedom from the life of bondage! Let us continually protect and guard our hearts from evil with all vigilance.

Have a freeing day!

!

Day 253
KILLING GREED AND FOSTERING SATISFACTION

Greed can take us down a dangerous path and the bible tells us to kill greed and desire.

Exodus 20:17 You shall not covet your neighbor's house, your neighbors wife, or his maidservant, or his ox, or his donkey, or anything that is your neighbor's.

God tells us not to desire our neighbors' goods because it leads us to feel unfulfilled from the comparisons we make. We must learn to be content with what God has given. The grass is not greener on the other side.

Philippians 4:11 Not that I am implying that I was in any personal want, for I have learned how to be content (satisfied to the point where I am not disturbed or disquieted) in whatever state I am.

We must not be like children, always wanting more. It takes a spiritual maturity to learn to be content. We need the inner satisfaction in knowing God and being His child.

1 Timothy 6:6 (And it is indeed, a source of immense profit, for) godliness accompanied with contentment (that contentment which is a sense of inward sufficiency) is great and abundant gain.

We must come to a place of being satisfied with what God wants us to have. He knows us perfectly and knows what we can or cannot handle. Let us find the peace, happiness and contentment in our lives as gifts from God.

Have a grateful day!

Day 254
DO NOT WASTE YOUR LIFE

There is so much in life to experience! What a shame it would be to let it go to waste and not take on the opportunities given to us.

Luke 7:31-32 To what then can I compare the people of this generation? What are they like? They are like children sitting in the marketplace and calling out to each other: "We played the flute for you, and you did not dance; we sang a dirge, and you did not cry."

I pray that we are not ones to allow life to pass us by. There are way too many relationships, activities, productive work, celebrations, beauty, etc., in life to enjoy! The reason Jesus came is to give us an abundant life!

John 10:10 I came that they may have and enjoy life, and have it in abundance (to the full, till it overflows).

Now then when we hear lively music, let us dance, when we hear sorrow and wailing, let us weep. Let us be encouraged to experience every part of life given to us, by Jesus coming into this world for *our benefit*!

Have a meaningful day!

Day 255
TO BE AWE-STRUCK

Do you want to be wowed and in awe? There are things that are hidden, but will be shown unto you when you call upon God!

Jeremiah 33:3 Call to Me and I will answer you and show you great and mighty things, fenced in and hidden, which you do not know (do not distinguish and recognize, have knowledge of and understand.

God has so many great and wonderful things in store for us! When we fear and revere Him, calling His name, His blessings, plans and purposes will be revealed in due time! We must stay in faith and trust Him completely in all matters of our life! First call and wait and look to God for answers and revelations in your life! When it is revealed, you will definitely be in awe and marveled!

Have an awe-struck day!

Day 256
ESCAPING TEMPTATION

How do we deal with temptation? We may think that we are the only ones dealing with temptation but no one can escape it. We are not alone, but God does provide a way out but it is our choice to take it or not.

1 Corinthians 10:13 For no temptation has overtaken you and laid hold on you that is not common to man (that is, no temptation or trial has come to you that is beyond human resistance and that is not adjusted and adapted and belonging to human experience, and such as man can bear). But God is faithful, and He (can be trusted) not to let you be tempted and tried and assayed beyond your ability and strength of resistance and power to endure, but with the temptation He will (always) also provide the way out (the means of escape to a landing place), that you may be capable and strong and powerful to bear up under it patiently.

So there is no need to worry when temptation strikes now knowing that everyone goes through it and there is a way of escape. Let us take action and move toward the exit sign of escape that God provides as we trust in His faithfulness, deliverance, and His promises to us. Putting our fear and reverence in God keeps us in line. Let us rely on His strength and might to flee and lead us out.

Have a take-action day!

Day 257
A SURE WINNER AGAINST EVIL

God gives us a distinct and a clear answer for times when we are facing the enemy.

Romans 12:21 Do not let yourself be overcome by evil, but overcome (master) evil with good.

It can't get any more plain and simple than that. It is, by far, a sure-fire winner against evil. Our natural human tendency pushes us to avenge pain inflicted upon us. Instead, leave the pain, disappointment and animosity to God and allow Him to deal with it. God wants us to rise above. By being His child we represent love in a higher form. If God is love, and His Spirit dwells within us, we should emit love from every part of our being. Remember, it is not about "me, myself and I," but rather about intentionally expressing God's love so we can be used by Him in a greater way than we can ever imagine. Let us pray for wisdom and guidance in this area of great challenge to be more Christ-like, winning God's approval. Tremendous blessings always overflow with kindness.

Have a good day!

TO BE BLESSED?

A common phrase we use is "God bless you!" But what does it mean to be blessed? I'm sure we would all like to be blessed.

Numbers 6:22-26 And the Lord said to Moses, Say to Aaron and his sons, This is the way you shall bless the Israelites. Say to them, The Lord bless you and watch, guard, and keep you; The Lord make His face to shine upon and enlighten you and be gracious (kind, merciful, and giving favor) to you; The Lord lift up His (approving) countenance upon you and give you peace (tranquility of heart and life continually).

Wow! To be blessed is beyond magnificent. Who wouldn't want to be blessed all their life? With God's blessings upon us, we can face life issues head on with all confidence, knowing that God is on our side to protect, guide and help us in every need with a smiling face. He'll give us the unsurpassed peace all throughout our journey of life in the midst of hardships and joy! Let us be one to have a happy, glowing countenance, knowing that we are truly blessed!

Have a blessed day!

Day 259
TIMELY HELP

Why is it that we really think that we can handle all our problems, temptations, and challenges all by ourselves? The sooner we go to God confidently to help us, the better off we will be!

Hebrews 4:16 Let us then fearlessly and confidently and boldly draw near to the throne of grace (the throne of God's unmerited favor to us sinners), that we may receive mercy (for our failures) and find grace to help in good time for every need (appropriate help and well-timed help, coming just when we need it).

Our help, support, comfort, and victory is right there available to us. All we have to do is draw near to God and ask Him for help. Wouldn't we want to simply ask, rather than be stagnant in misery? Allow God to intercede for you today.

Have an asking day!

Day 260
BE CONVINCED OF GOD'S PROMISES

What does it take to convince you of God's promises in your life? Doubt always seems to creep up when dealing with the challenges of hardships and pain. It is crucial that we look back and remember God helping us through our past issues.

Romans 4:20-21 Abraham never wavered in believing God's promise. In fact, his faith grew stronger, and in this he brought glory to God. He was absolutely convinced that God was able to do anything God promised.

How convinced are you? What does it take to shake up your own faith in God -- for it to grow and blossom? God did the impossible by giving Abraham a son that he requested at the old age of 100. We must believe that God can work the impossible in our lives as well. We cannot limit God in anything for His thoughts, plans and ways are higher than ours. Let us give God all glory and praise by believing in His promises to us.

Have a faith-filled day!

Day 261
A TRUTH THAT IS HARD TO GRASP

It's a truth that is hard to grasp, but God's will for you is greater than the sufferings and trials in your life.

1 Peter4:1-2 So, since Christ suffered in the flesh for us, for you, arm yourselves with the same thought and purpose (patiently to suffer than fail to please God). For whoever has suffered in the flesh is done with sin (has stopped pleasing himself and the world, and pleases God), So that he can no longer spend the rest of his natural life living by (his) human appetites and desires, but for what God wills.

Notice during times of suffering, all we think about are ourselves. We may think "it's not fair" and "why me?" There is a greater reason why it is you who are facing these trials or obstacles. There is a plan for you that is part of God's will! Let's be in agreement with God, knowing He is with us. Let us not fail in pleasing Him. May we trust that nothing but good results will come of our faith and agreement to His will!

Romans 8:18 For I consider that the sufferings of this present time are not worth being compared with the glory that is about to be revealed to us and in us and for us and conferred on us.

Your glory will outshine your dark, dark days.

Have a faith-filled day!

Day 262
GOD LISTENS, ACCORDING TO HIS WILL

There is a way to know for sure that God will hear and listen to our requests: If they are aligned with His will and with His plans.

1 John 5:14 And this is the confidence which we have in Him: (we are sure) that if we ask anything (make any request) according to His will (in agreement with His own plan), He listens to and hears us.

When we have children, wouldn't we want to give them what they want according to our plan and purposes for their lives? If they ramble about asking selfishly for this or that, we may put on a deaf ear and tune them out! Let us trust in God's ways and in His timing patiently to give us what we ask for, if it is according to His will. To learn and find out God's will in our life is through His word.

Psalm 119:105 Your word is a lamp to my feet and a light to my path.

Being in God's will and running His course in your life is where you want to be! That is a fulfilled life full of peace and joy!

Have a discerning day!

Day 263
WE HAVE ALL SINNED

We should definitely not point a finger at others and their sin, for we all have sinned, in one way or another, whether small or grievous. God only knows.

Romans 3:23 For everyone has sinned; we all fall short of God's glorious standard.

That is why God sent Jesus to die on the cross, for all of our sins, to redeem us and to be made right with Him.

Romans 3:24 (All) are justified and made upright and in right standing with God, freely and gratuitously by His grace, (His unmerited favor and mercy), through the redemption which is (provided) in Christ Jesus, Whom God put forward (before the eyes of all) as a mercy seat and propitiation by His blood (the cleansing and life-giving sacrifice of atonement and reconciliation, to be received) through faith. This was to show God's righteousness, because in His divine forbearance He had passed over and ignored former sins without punishment.

Can you imagine how many times we would have been punished for our sins? Thank goodness God ignores our sins when we ask for forgiveness through Jesus. What an awesome God we have. The next time you want to take the speck out of your brother's eyes, first look at the plank in your own eyes. Praise God for His love, mercy and grace.

Have a pondering day!

Day 264
WHY ARE WE NEGATIVE ALL THE TIME?

Are you at a place where you are negative, complaining and moaning all the time? Why are we negative all the time? The way you think greatly affects how you feel.

Psalm 55:2 Attend to me and answer me; I am restless and distraught in my complaint and must moan.

We must change the way we think in order to be set free from this agony of negativity. God tells us the importance to renew our minds in Him. Once we see everything in and through God's eyes, by changing our perspective, our behavior will automatically change.

Psalm 55:6 And I say, Oh, that I had wings like a dove! I would fly away and be at rest.

If you desire to fly and to be free, the key is to put our rest in God.

Psalm 55:22 Cast your burden on the Lord (releasing the weight of it) and He will sustain you; He will never allow the (consistently) righteous to be moved (made to slip, fall, or fail).

There is no need to worry or have anxieties because God is going to take care of you for He cares for you affectionately and cares about you watchfully. Take comfort in that.

Have a free thinking day!

Day 265
GOD KNOWS YOU INTIMATELY

God knows you inside and out! How personalized is this?

Psalm 139:1-10 O Lord, you have searched me and you know me. You know when I sit and when I rise; you perceive my thoughts from afar. You discern my going out and my lying down; you are familiar with all my ways. Before a word is on my tongue you know it completely, O Lord. You hem me in-behind and before; you have laid Your hand upon me. Such knowledge is too wonderful for me, too lofty for me to attain. Where can I go from your Spirit? Where can I flee from Your presence? If I go up to the heavens, you are there; if I make my bed in the depths, you are there. If I rise on the wings of the dawn, if I settle on the far side of the sea, even there your hand will guide me, Your right hand will hold me fast.

Now, if you feel that nobody knows and understands you, God surely does and loves you with all His being! Take comfort in that; it is wonderful to know that we can put our trust in someone who knows us better than we know ourselves.

Have an assured day!

Day 266
YOU ARE CHOSEN

In God's eyes, we are not just a number. We are loved by Him, we are very special to Him, and we are specifically chosen by Him to do good works in our lives. He chose us in every area of our lives to be, for example: parents to our children, partners for our spouses, trained in tasks or work we do in home or at our jobs, volunteer work, etc., to help and fulfill His plans and purposes in our lives and the people surrounding us.

1 Thessalonians 1:4 (O) brethren beloved by God, we recognize and know that He has selected (chosen) you.

You have a great purpose and are chosen. Pray that God will help to reveal your purpose in all that you do! Thank God that He loves you and has chosen and selected you.

Have a privileged day!

Day 267
DON'T JUST SIT THERE AND COMPLAIN

It can be difficult to give up on difficult circumstances that seem hopeless. God wants us to do our part in rising up and then He'll do His part. Just have faith.

2 Kings 7:3-7 Now there were four men with leprosy at the entrance of the city gate. They said to each other, "Why stay here until we die? If we say, 'We'll go into the city' -- the famine is there, and we will die. And if we stay here, we will die. So let's go over to the camp of the Arameans and surrender. If they spare us, we live; if they kill us, then we die. At dusk they got up and went to the camp of the Arameans. When they reached the edge of the camp, not a man was there, for the Lord had caused the Arameans to hear the sound of chariots and horses and a great army, so that they said to one another. "Look, the king of Israel has hired the Hittite and Egyptian kings to attack us!" So they got up and fled in the dusk and abandoned their tents and their horses and donkeys. They left the camp as it was and ran for their lives.

See what God can do? He made the enemies think that they had been defeated and they ran for their lives. If we always shrink back in fear and don't do our part, then we miss out on God's glory. If we want God to move in our lives, don't just sit there and complain and feel sorry for yourselves. Let's do what we can do and allow God to do what we cannot do.

Have a faith-action day!

Day 268
WE ARE THE HOME OF THE SPIRIT

A house has many different rooms; the living room, kitchen, bathroom, etc.. We go to each room for different reasons and we have great comfort in our house. Did you know as a believer in Christ that the Holy Spirit makes His home in us?

2 Timothy 1:14 Guard and keep (with the greatest care) the precious and excellently adapted (Truth) which has been entrusted (to you), by the (help of the) Holy Spirit Who makes His home in us.

The Spirit of God helps us with guarding His word and truth within us. The Spirit protects your heart from evil by guiding your feet in which direction to go, and protects your mind, helping you work with your hands productively.

Allow the Spirit who resides in you to freely go in every room of your home and be useful in the areas that you need help. Protect the truth that is within you by the help and support of the Spirit!

Have a Spirit-filled day!

Day 269
PAY ATTENTION AND KEEP FOCUSED

We should train our minds to pay attention and to keep focused on what we are doing!

Ecclesiastes 5:1 Keep your foot (give mind to what you are doing).

It takes some time and discipline to stay on track in your mind or what you are doing. We can easily get distracted and wander, losing our focus and getting off balance in our mind and action. When we keep our eyes fixed on God, we will not lose our balance! If our eyes are away from God, worries, anxieties, and unsettledness can all creep within us and set us off track in all things in our lives.

It is so important to learn and train yourself to be aware. Pay attention to what you are doing; starting with your thought-life can lead you to great peace, comfort, direction and a truly fulfilled life. Let us pray that the Spirit will help us in our training to keep our balance!

Have a balanced day!

Day 270
REMEMBER GOD'S FAITHFULNESS

Can we really truly grasp the faithfulness of our God?

1 Thessalonians 5:24 Faithful is He Who is calling you (to Himself) and utterly trustworthy, and He will also do it (fulfill His call by hallowing and keeping you).

People can often let us down in many ways, but our Almighty God keeps and holds on to His promises for us! The promises to protect, provide, promote and to prosper you in so many other numerous things! Why? Because He loves you! He woos us unto Himself, to know Him and develop a relationship with Him. He never will let us down in any way, and only wants what is the best for us!

Even though we may let Him down with our imperfections, it doesn't surprise Him one bit! He created us and knows us inside and out. He is trustworthy, reliable, stable, and will never leave us or forsake us. The song says, "Great is Thy faithfulness! Morning by morning new mercies I see. All I have needed Thy hand hath provided; Great is Thy faithfulness, Lord, unto me!" It can't get any better than that, living in God's faithfulness!

Have a most secured day!

Day 271
SIMPLY CALL UPON GOD

Many times our stubbornness, laziness, rebellion, or maybe just a lack of faith prevents us to simply call upon God in times of need.

Psalm 91:15 He will call upon Me, and I will answer him; I will be with him in trouble, I will deliver him and honor him.

Why do we think that we can handle things all by ourselves? We are not made for that! God created us so that we become aware of the void within us that only He can fill. Let us be encouraged to habitually and simply go to God in prayer for everything. He promises to help us, answer us, and deliver us! Be patient knowing and trusting that His timing and plans are intricately detailed in every area of your life!

Have a prayer filled day!

OUCH! IT HURTS SO GOOD

What does it mean exactly to hurt so *good*? It means no pain, no gain, for our goodness!

Hebrews 12:5-7 My son, do not make light of the Lord's discipline, and do not lose heart when He rebukes you, because the Lord disciplines those He loves, and He punishes everyone He accepts as a son. Endure hardship as discipline; God is treating you as sons. For what son is not disciplined by his father?

Think of a parent disciplining for the children's own good, because they love them so and want what is best for them, to teach their children to go in the right direction!

Hebrews 12:10-11 Our fathers disciplined us for a little while as they thought best; but God disciplines us for our good, that we may share in His holiness. No discipline seems pleasant at the time, but painful. Later on, however, it produces a harvest of righteousness and peace for those who have been trained by it.

Let us look at our pain and trials as loving discipline from God our Father and not resist, but know that it is for our own good. Our sovereign God has a good plan for you. Yield and trust in Him today!

Have a good day!

Day 273
DOING GOOD EQUALS A PEACEFUL HEART

We all know the difference between good and evil but why is it so hard to do good? Why does evil seem so inviting and fun? Remember that doing good equals a peaceful heart. Outwardly peace comes from knowing God on the inside.

Romans 2:10 But glory and honor and (heart) peace shall be awarded to everyone who (habitually) does good.

What is a habit? A habit is something we start and build up gradually that eventually becomes automatic for us. It could be brushing our teeth, taking a daily walk, driving the same route to work, and so much more. God wants us to build up a habit of thinking and doing good. Great rewards shall be ours when we put doing good into daily practice. Give it a try and see your life change for the better.

Have a good day!

Day 274
HONORING GOD IN COMMUNICATION

The art of communication is so important and vital in developing healthy relationships. The bible even warns us to limit our speech.

Proverbs 10:19   When words are many, sin is not absent, but he who holds his tongue is wise.

Talking too much can get us into trouble. We must learn to discipline and control our mouths on what to say.

Ephesians 4:29   Let no foul or polluting language, nor evil word nor unwholesome or worthless talk (ever) come out of your mouth, but only such (speech) as is good and beneficial to the spiritual progress of others, as is fitting to the need and the occasion, that it may be a blessing and give grace (God's favor) to those who hear it.

To build good, loving and edifying relationships with our spouses, children, coworkers, friends, etc.., we must practice the art of focused listening and wise speech -- think before you speak. Words are so powerful. Anything said and heard cannot be rescinded and undone so let us pray for wisdom and discernment in our talk so that God will be honored in all that we do and say. Good relationships with people are a part of enjoying your life. Let us build each other up in the kingdom of God.

Have a thought-provoking day!

Day 275
WHERE DO YOU PUT YOUR FOCUS

Where do you put your focus? It is very important to put our focus on Jesus. Otherwise, fears and faults come in and harass us.

Matthew 17:8 And when they raised their eyes, they saw no one but Jesus.

Who do you see when you are afraid or have doubts and disappointments? When we give our focus to Jesus, all that distracts us go away and we remember the power of Jesus' death on the cross for us and are reminded of His unceasing great love, sacrifice, protection and fulfillment. When we remember who we are to God, we are comforted by the Father, our Shepherd, who is faithful to always guide, protect, provide and strengthen us. He brings us to a place of peace and joy. Let us look up only to Jesus and put our faith and trust in Him alone. Rely on God and in His promises to be true and effective. That is where victory is to be found.

Have a most focused day!

Day 276
TEMPTATION AGAIN? WHAT SHOULD WE DO?

How many times do we kick ourselves, not wanting to fall into temptation, and to walk along with a good right spirit? But our flesh can take over, and that itself is our weakness!

Mark 14:38   Keep awake and watch and pray (constantly), that you may not enter into temptation; the spirit indeed is willing, but the flesh is weak.

It is very important for us to always pray not to give into temptation. Prayer is powerful and effective, and it is vital that we are in sync with God and His Spirit when we do pray. Prayer opens the door for God to work in our lives.

Romans 7:20-21   Now if I do what I do not desire to do, it is no longer I doing it, but the sin which dwells within me (fixed and operating in my soul). So I find it to be a law that when I want to do what is right and good, evil is ever present with me and I am subject to its insistent demands.

Let us shield ourselves from the fiery darts of temptations. With the power of prayer, we have the choice not to give into them! Use your better judgment and stay away from anyone, tempting environment and keep away from situations that will easily lead you to sin.

Have a strengthening day!

WE ARE SELECTED AND ADOPTED BY GOD

Just as grocery shoppers hand-pick fruits and vegetables and just as athletic teams select the best players, God has picked and chosen us to be adopted as His own children through Christ Jesus.

Ephesians 1:4-5   Even as (in His love) He chose us (actually picked us out for Himself as His own) in Christ before the foundation of the world, that we should be holy (consecrated and set apart for Him) and blameless in His sight, even above reproach, before Him in love. For He foreordained us (destined us, planned in love for us) to be adopted (revealed as His own children through Jesus Christ, in accordance with the purpose of His will (because it pleased Him and was His kind intent).

We please God in every manner. He created us so that He may enjoy us. It pleases Him, as His children, that we are set apart to do His good will and purpose. God is so good and His kindness reigns. We should thank God for the privilege to be picked out and adopted by Him. Know that you are special, loved and valuable in God's eyes. He knows that we make mistakes but we can be forgiven through Christ Jesus. Let us stay on our God given path and bring Him purposeful glory.

Have a valued day!

Day 278
WHAT SEASON ARE YOU IN?

Each year, we experience the seasons of Winter, Spring, Summer and Fall. As we know, there are also different seasons in life. What season of life are you in right now?

Ecclesiastes 3:1 To everything there is a season, and a time for every matter or purpose under heaven.

If you are in a good season, then enjoy and be thankful with a grateful heart to the fullest. Maybe you are in a challenging, difficult season; in that case, remember that this too shall pass and God promises to be with you through it all.

Romans 8:18 For I consider that the sufferings of this present time are not worth being compared with the glory that is about to be revealed to us and in us and for us and conferred on us!

This means, whatever hardship that we are going through right now cannot be compared to whatever glory that will soon be revealed to us in due time, more than we can imagine! Stay in faith today and keep on keeping on.

Ecclesiastes 3:11 He has made everything beautiful in its time.

Trust in God no matter what, because He has His eye upon you!

Have a peaceful day!

Day 279
TO BE IN GOD'S CONTINUAL PRESENCE

How can we not have peace, comfort and security when we know our God and His character? In the midst of trials, disasters, and tribulations, seeking God's presence is where we want to be!

Ecclesiastes 8:12 Though a sinner does evil a hundred times and his days are prolonged (in his wickedness), yet surely I know that It will be well with those who (reverently) fear God, who revere and worship Him, realizing His continual presence.

God deeply desires to fellowship with us.

Psalm 25:13-14 He himself shall dwell At ease, and his offspring shall inherit the land. The secret (of the sweet, satisfying companionship) of the Lord have they who FEAR (revere and worship) Him, and He will show them His covenant and reveal to them its (deep, inner) meaning.

When people question your true peace during hard times, it is only between you and your constant fellowship with Him, that He has shown you great and meaningful insight. Let us desire to be continually in God's presence everyday of our lives.

Have an uplifting day!

Day 280
CHECK YOURSELF BEFORE YOU
IMMEDIATELY RESPOND

It takes some discipline on our part to not immediately say or do something rash, without thinking it out first. We must think before we speak!

Acts 19:36 Seeing then that these things cannot be denied, you ought to be quiet (keep yourselves in check) and do nothing rashly.

There is wisdom and maturity involved in this manner. We may wonder why we can say or do things, and commit to certain obligations that can easily lead towards pressure, frustration and stress. We simply don't think things through before we speak. There is nothing wrong when asked a question, to say "I'll think about it" before giving a direct answer. That way we can ponder and see if it will work with our schedule, health, lifestyle, or our faith. Let us pray for wisdom and discernment in this area to have a peaceful, healthy and fulfilled life! Be encouraged to check yourself before you immediately respond.

Have a no-nonsense day!

Day 281
LISTENING TO YOUR GOD-GIVEN CONSCIENCE

We all seem to have a conscience, but as believers, let us be led by the Holy Spirit which directs our conscience with God's word and His truth. Our conscience is like a radar and it signals what is right and what is displeasing to God. The Spirit activates our conscience and leads us toward the right direction. If we choose to ignore our conscience, it eventually becomes quiet, resulting in a life of disaster.

1 Timothy 1:19 Holding fast to faith (that leaning of the entire human personality on God in absolute trust and confidence) and having a good (clear) conscience. By rejecting and thrusting from them (their conscience), some individuals have made shipwreck of their faith.

Beware! If you notice that your faith is diminishing, maybe it's time to reactivate and sensitize your conscience through the Holy Spirit's power. It is very important to keep our conscience crystal clear and allow it to detect any harm thrown our way. The more we learn about God and His word of truth, the more ability we gain to know which direction to go. As we listen to our God-given conscience, we will continue to walk in our right path with God through the journey of our lives with His presence.

Have a sensitive day!

Day 282
WHAT DO I HAVE TO OFFER?

There may be times when we think to ourselves, "What do I have to offer?" When we see people in need, we can be hesitant in offering our gifts and talents, money, time, etc.. because we think what we offer is small and petty. Think again. God can use our small offerings and make them big and gigantic for His kingdom's use.

Matthew 14:16-21 Jesus replied, "They do not need to go away. You give them something to eat." "We have here only five loaves of bread and two fish," they answered. "Bring them here to me," he said. And he directed the people to sit down on the grass. Taking the five loaves and the two fish and looking up to heaven, he gave thanks and broke the loaves. Then he gave them to the disciples, and the disciples gave them to the people. They all ate and were satisfied, and the disciples picked up twelve basket fulls of broken pieces that were left over. The number of those who ate was about five thousand men, besides women and children.

There is no excuse and what you have to offer is worth more than you think. Believe and trust that God can take whatever you can offer and make miracles from them. God's power shows up greater in our weakness. Let us not doubt what God can do for He makes all things possible with our small offerings.

Have a significant day!

Day 283
IMITATE GOD OUR FATHER

Notice the similarities between our fathers and our Heavenly Father! The main goal of being a good parent and role model for our children is to represent God, our Father, in a good loving way!

Ephesians 6:4 Fathers, do not irritate and provoke your children to anger (do not exasperate them to resentment), but rear them (tenderly) in the training and discipline and the counsel and admonition of the Lord.

Let us imitate God our Father by looking to Jesus' character and how He lived. That best describes who God is and also represents the pathway to a relationship with God. As we know and follow the Heavenly Father, we will be the parents He designed us to be for our own children. We can establish a right relationship with them and be a role model of our God in love! There are many traits of the Heavenly Father we can imitate, such as His love and sacrifice for us, His provision, protection, gentleness, kindness, friendship, being disciplinarian in love and grace and so much more! Let us yield to God's Spirit to help guide and enable us each day in wisdom to be the godly parent to our children!

Have an establishing day!

Day 284
GOD'S SPIRIT SPEAKING FOR YOU

Is there a time when you feel inadequate on what to say appropriately? Let us not look too much from within our capabilities, but rather put our trust and faith in God who is the source and maker of our mouths.

Exodus 3:12   Now go; I will help you speak and will teach you what to say.

Moses felt inadequate in his lack of speech on what to say in order to lead the Israelites out of Egypt. God told him not to worry because He would help him on what to say at the given time. Yielding our spirit to God's, He will help us say what needs to be said. You will be truly amazed what comes out of your mouth, because you know it wasn't you, but God's Spirit speaking for you!

We should not worry or fear when we have to confront or talk to others; such as a certain someone you may have issues with a spouse, co worker, friend, parent etc.. Pray and allow God to speak through you!

Have a mind-blowing day!

Day 285
GOD CAN USE YOU IN AND AT THE UNLIKELIEST PLACE

Sometimes when we are at the lowest points in our state of mind, circumstances or situations, God can still use you to bring Him glory and *free* you at the same time!

Acts 16:25-31 ...Paul and Silas were praying and singing hymns to God, and the other prisoners were listening to them. Suddenly there was such a violent earthquake that the foundations of the prison were shaken. At once all the prison doors flew open, and everybody's chains came loose. The jailer woke up, and when he saw the prison doors open, he drew his sword and was about to kill himself because he thought the prisoners had escaped. But Paul shouted, "Don't harm yourself! We are all here!" The jailer...fell trembling before Paul and Silas. He then brought them out and asked, "Sirs, what must I do to be saved?

Wow! What an opportunity for Paul and Silas to witness to the other prisoners and the jailer to know and believe in God, and in prison of all places! You never know how God can use you in and at the unlikeliest places. Believe that God can do the impossible any moment in your life. Never feel defeated! Instead, rejoice because victory is right around the corner. Stay in faith!

Have a miraculous day!

Day 286
RECEIVING WISDOM

There is a way to receive wisdom: by listening to God. When God rebukes us, it is important to turn, repent and respond to His reproach. Then He will pour out His heart to us and make His thoughts known to us.

Proverbs 1:23 If you will turn (repent) and give heed to my reproof, behold, I (Wisdom) will pour out my spirit upon you.

If we choose to resist God and not listen to Him, we invite calamity, distress and anguish. God's ways are better than our own. Every day, let us trust in Him for direction.

Proverbs 3:5-6 Lean on, trust in. and be confident in the Lord with all your heart and mind and do not rely on your own insight or understanding. In all your ways know, recognize, and acknowledge Him, and He will direct and make straight and plain your paths.

All we have to do is put aside our own thoughts, ways and ideas and lean on God for everything. He will then come through in giving you wisdom to direct you.

Have a wise day!

Day 287
FIGHTING THE GOOD FIGHT

We cannot know the full extent of our character until we are met with hardship. Refinement comes through tests and struggles.

Deuteronomy 8:2 And you shall (earnestly) remember all the way which the Lord your God led you these forty years in the wilderness, to humble you and to prove you, to know what was in your (mind and) heart, whether you would keep His commandments or not.

There is the great challenge of keeping God's word and commandments when we are in the long period of tough times through our weariness and disheartened condition! We may think that we will never get through and out of the wilderness but let us have hope and never give up. God has a great plan for you. Stay in faith and keep persistent. Our character is being built up immensely for His glory if we only stay in faith and trust in Him. To hear God say, "Well done my good and faithful servant," is priceless.

Have an enduring day!

Day 288
LEARN TO TRUST GOD COMPLETELY

Where are you at in believing God's promises to you? Are you still unsure that God will keep His promises in your life or have you grown to a full assurance from past events that God will surely keeps his promises?

Romans 4:18-21 Against all hope, Abraham in hope believed and so became the father of many nations, just as it had been said to him, "So shall your offspring be." Without weakening in his faith, he faced the fact that his body was as good as dead-since he was about a hundred years old-and that Sarah's womb was also dead. Yet he did not waver through unbelief regarding the promise of God, but was strengthened in his faith and gave glory to God, being fully persuaded that God had power to do what he had promised.

My goodness, Abraham was against all odds and reason, he and Sarah being so old to bear any children! Instead, he never wavered in believing God's promise, In fact, his faith grew stronger and in this he brought glory to God. He was absolutely convinced that God was able to do anything He promised. Let us also look to God and believe in His promises even if things don't always make sense at first. Trust in His time, He will make all things beautiful!

Have a hopeful day!

Day 289
WHAT JUST HIT US?

As believers, it is very important not to allow ourselves to be triggered with hate, jealousy, anger or any kind of animosity toward other people or situation in life. Instead, know and acknowledge that the driving force comes from our enemy.

Ephesians 6:10-12 Finally, be strong in the Lord and in His mighty power. Put on the full armor of God so that you can take your stand against the devil's schemes. For our struggle is not against flesh and blood, but against the rulers, against the authorities, against the powers of this dark world and against the spiritual forces of evil in the heavenly realms.

The main goal is to keep on standing. Our enemy wants to see us fall and he'll use any means to make that eventually happen. Be aware! Negativity is used intricately, with well-laid plans, to bring us down to destruction. Starting out small in our minds, it influences us through our actions to lead us away from our right path towards evil. It's subtle and deceitful ways can strike when we're vulnerable, and if we don't guard and protect ourselves, we wouldn't know just what hit us.

Have a firm, strong standing day!

Day 290
EMBRACE EACH NEW DAY

Notice how each new day gives us hope for a new beginning? Let us embrace each new day. God gives us His mercy and loving kindness every morning.

Lamentations 3:21-23 But this I recall and therefore have hope and expectation: It is because of the Lord's mercy and loving-kindness that we are not consumed, because His (tender) compassions fail not. They are new every morning; great and abundant is Your stability and faithfulness.

God is faithful with His promises to you. He gives new love and mercy each day. Even though we make mistakes or dwell on our own problems, after a good night's sleep, God offers us newness. Just as God gives us His mercy, let us also give out mercy to others with love and forgiveness. Let us thank God for His great and abundant mercy. God never changes and He is our stability. Great is thy faithfulness our God almighty. Praise God!

Have an embracing day!

Day 291
WHAT IS THE ARMOR OF GOD?

It is very important that we keep our spiritual life active and alert at all times, because the enemy desires for us to fall into destruction. We need to stand firm with the whole armor of God! But what is the armor of God?

Ephesians 6:14-18   Stand firm then, with the belt of truth buckled around your waist, with the breastplate of righteousness in place, and with your feet fitted with the readiness that comes from the gospel of peace. In addition to all this, take up the shield of faith, with which you can extinguish all the flaming arrows of the evil one. Take the helmet of salvation and the sword of the spirit, which is the word of God.

Along with this, pray, and keep on praying. As we in Spirit daily put on the armor of God, we will always conquer the enemy in victory. Let us make a daily habit to consciously "wear" God's armor today, and every day! Remember who you are a child of God. So, let us stand in faith and truth victoriously!

Have a conquering day!

Day 292
AN OPEN HEART AND MIND BRINGS
UNDERSTANDING

Even though we may think we know God, we may not truly understand all that He's trying to say and teach us.

Acts 16:14 One of those listening was a woman named Lydia, a dealer in purple cloth from the city of Thyatira, who was a worshiper of God. The Lord opened her heart to respond to Paul's message.

She responded by receiving the word of salvation from Paul's message! She and her household were saved, baptized, and invited Paul to her home. The importance of an open heart is crucial to learning new things that God wants to teach us. If our hearts are closed, there will be no room for growth in a life full of freedom and joy! We will not understand where people are coming from and why certain situations come about in our lives.

Luke 24:45 Then He (Jesus) opened their minds so they could understand the scriptures.

When we hear God's word speaking to us, let us pray that God will open our hearts and minds to fully and thoroughly understand all that He's saying and teaching us to give us life and peace in all areas of our lives!

Have an awakening day!

NO ONE IS EXCLUDED FROM THE GRACE OF GOD'S SALVATION

We shouldn't point fingers at others, saying "Oh, there is no way that person can be saved!" No one is excluded from the grace of God's salvation.

Acts 15:11   But we believe that we are saved through the grace (the undeserved favor and mercy) of the Lord Jesus, just as they are).

We shouldn't think for a moment that a person is saved because of his good works. No, we are all saved by grace! Jesus came to save all of us as *equals*! We all need His grace because of our imperfections and brokenness!

Acts 15:9   And He made no difference between us and them, but cleansed their hearts by faith (by a strong and welcome conviction that Jesus is the Messiah, through Whom, we obtain eternal salvation in the kingdom of God).

Praise God for His wonderful grace; without it we would all be completely lost! Let us accept and indulge in His grace everyday and give Him the praise and glory He deserves.

Have a thankful day!

Day 294
THE HELP OF *HIND'S FEET* THROUGH DIFFICULTIES

A *hind* is a type of mountain goat that can leap about freely on rocky, difficult slopes. Hinds climb mountains with such ease because of the way God has made them. Don't we all wish we can somehow maneuver throughout our struggles and challenges as the hinds do thru rocky terrain? God promises to give us *hind's feet* with His strength to help us through!

Habakkuk 3:19 Lord God is my Strength, my personal bravery, and my invincible army; He makes my feet like hinds' feet and will make me to walk (not to stand still in terror, but to walk) and make (spiritual) progress upon my high places (of trouble, suffering, or responsibility)!

Wow! God is right there with you with His power and might giving you *hind's feet*! God wants us to progress spiritually during hard times and to keep on moving forward. Don't get stuck or go backwards; use what is given to you and believe that with God you can succeed. See your obstacles as rocks to climb higher and higher!

Philippians 4:13 I can do all things through Christ who strengthens me.

Have a freeing day!

Day 295
SMALL MATTERS COUNT

There may be times when we think that small matters do not make a difference. Think twice. It makes a great deal in God's eyes. When we are faithful and trustworthy in every little thing, God can trust us with the big things in our lives.

Luke 19:17 'Well done, my good servant!' his master replied. 'Because you have been trustworthy in a very small matter, take charge of ten cities.'

Little things do count. Notice how our trust level grows when we see children, friends, spouses, etc.., keep their word and follow through with their actions. If they do not consistently do small things, we cannot trust them with handling and taking care of the large tasks given to them. Let us be aware and faithfully, earnestly and diligently do the small things God asks of us. The rewards and blessings are big in God's kingdom.

Have a take-notice day!

Day 296
JUDGING OTHERS

It is of great importance to have a clean and clear vision when we see others. When we have the particles in our own eyes, we can easily judge people in the wrong way.

Matthew 7:1-5 Do not judge, or you too will be judged. For in the same way you judge others, you will be judged, and with the measure you use, it will be measured to you. Why do you look at the speck of sawdust in your brother's eye and pay no attention to the plank in your own eye? How can you say to your brother, 'Let me take the speck out of your eye,' when all the time there is a plant in your own eye? You hypocrite, first take the plank out of your own eye, and then you will see clearly to remove the speck from your brother's eye.

We have to meet ourselves and allow God to deal with us first through His Spirit, and then we will be able to clearly and lovingly help others in the right manner. Let us curve our outwardly pointing index finger and ask God to humbly work within us before we outstretc.h it towards others.

Have a right-spirit day!

Day 297
GOD MAKES ALL THINGS NEW

Have you been feeling stuck in a rut lately? God makes all things new!

Revelations 21:5 And He Who is seated on the throne said, See! I make all things new.

Isaiah 41:18-19 Do not (earnestly) remember the former things; neither consider the things of old. Behold, I am doing a new thing! Now it springs forth; do you not perceive and know it and will you not give heed to it? I will even make a way in the wilderness and rivers in the desert.

God is all about progression, newness, excitement and life! God will provide new opportunities for us! We just have to take him up on His offer and be bold enough to try new things. Do not allow fear to creep in, but trust that God wants good things for us. Make no excuses, but be aligned in agreement with God's will for you. If we choose to stay stagnant, we will never have the freedom to take on new opportunities with growth and joy. The choice is up to you! There is so much beauty in life, and we make it exciting by choosing to take it on with all God has to offer.

Have a progressive day!

STOP CHASING THE WIND! BE FULFILLED IN GOD

Why is it that we don't get full satisfaction from what life has to offer us? We put all our energy and time investing into people, jobs, or material goods…all for what? It is like trying to chase the wind, or a dog running around in circles trying to catch his tail! It is never ending and can be very tiresome!

Ecclesiastes 1:14 I have seen all the works that are done under the sun, and behold, all is vanity, a striving after the wind and a feeding on wind.

The wise King Solomon had it all! He knew that life was meaningless without knowing God. Our true fulfillment comes from knowing and fearing God with obedience to Him! All of life's meaning is directed towards being in a right relationship with God our Father. Fulfillment is found as He is in our midst and motivation for all that we do.

Ecclesiastes 12:13 All has been heard; the end of the matter is: Fear God and keep His commandments, for this is the whole of man and the whole (duty) for every man.

Have a true, purposeful day!

Day 299
GOD, THE PROVIDER, ALWAYS

One thing is an absolute guarantee: God will never forsake nor leave us. It is important not to allow greed to take over. We must learn to be satisfied with our lives now.

Hebrews 13:5 Let your character or moral disposition be free from love of money (including greed, avarice, lust, and craving for earthly possessions) and be satisfied with your present (circumstances and with what you have); for He (God) Himself has said, I will not in any way fail you nor give you up nor leave you without support. (I will) not, (I will) not, (I will) not in any degree leave you helpless nor forsake nor let (you) down (relax My hold on you)! (Assuredly not!)

God is always in our presence and He will never abandon us in any way. Even amidst unforeseeable troubles, God is present to support us. We must believe that God does not flee us, but His providence exists always. Let us learn to trust Him, lean, wait and rest on Him to come through for us. He has and always will.

Have an assured day!

Day 300
EMBRACE BIBLICAL WOMANHOOD

We women must learn to be strong, our character to be carved out by God in order to perform our tasks as biblical women.

Psalm 144:12 Then our sons in their youth will be like well-nurtured plants, and our daughters will be like pillars carved to adorn a palace.

A pillar exists to give support to the palace structure as it also adds beauty, creating an atmosphere to all who enter. Similarly, it is our role, as women, to support our family: husband, children, younger women and the community. It is a role that is found behind the scenes. It is not obvious, yet a quiet strength builds up all those who surround her. Through that supportive, connecting help real beauty shines. If, and when, we are weak, it can be immensely destructive. Loving and fearing God with all respect and reverence is the key to our blessedness.

Psalm 144:15 Blessed are the people of whom this is true; blessed are the people whose God is the Lord.

When we fix our eyes and look to God as our Almighty Lord and strength, as well as our intimate Friend and Father, then we are able to trust in Him to do His will in and through us by the carving of His hands. Let us be encouraged to be the strong pillar of support in wisdom.

Have a strong day!

Day 301
THE CORRUPTION OF EVIL
COMPANIONSHIPS

There are good reasons why parents tell their children to be careful of what kind of friends to make. They do not want you to be influenced and surrounded by manipulative people with evil thoughts and actions. We may think that we are invincible and will be fine, but God tells us to be aware and on guard.

1 Corinthians 15:33 Do not be so deceived and misled! Evil companionships (communion, associations) corrupt and deprave good manners and morals and character.

If we allow ourselves to continually hang around bad influences, before we know it we will start to think and behave like them! We are not immune to negative and evil forces. They can be very contagious! Let us be of good influence to others in a godly manner, setting up boundaries with discernment and wisdom. Pray that God will help you in this manner to have boldness in standing up for who you are, a child of God!

Have a discerning day!

Day 302
HOW THIRSTY ARE YOU?

Can you imagine being in a hot desert, or running in a race without a drink of water? If someone was to offer you water, wouldn't you automatically take the drink in relief and refreshment? It would be senseless not to take the drink our bodies so desperately need. God Himself offers us living water with no price attached.

Revelations 21:6 And He said to me, It is done! I am the Alpha and the Omega, the Beginning and the End. To the thirsty I (Myself) will give water without price from the fountain (springs) of the water of life.

God knows what you need! Trust in Him to provide all your needs one day at a time; it's free!

Isaiah 55:1 Wait and listen, everyone who is thirsty! Come to the waters; and he who has no money, come, but and eat! Yes, come, buy (priceless, spiritual) wine and milk without money and without price (simply for the self-surrender that accepts the blessings).

God offers a rich and blessed life! It'll be senseless to refuse His offer of living water! Let us be encouraged to receive His ultimate refreshment and bask in it today.

Have a quenching day!

Day 303
FATHER OF LIES

Oh my goodness! Just think about having a father that is a liar, where everything about him is false. How awful is that! The enemy is the father of lies.

John 8:44 You are of your father, the devil, and it is your will to practice the lusts and gratify the desires (which are characteristic) of your father. He was a murderer from the beginning and does not stand in the truth, because there is no truth in him. When he speaks a falsehood, he speaks what is natural to him, For he is a liar and father of lies and of all that is false.

We belong to a God of truth! Know who you truly are and where you stand. Do not allow yourselves to be deceived by the enemy's schemes and lies. All the negative feelings, thoughts and actions come from our enemy! The more we know the word of God and His truth, we will be able to detect a lie.

John 8:32 And you will know the truth, and the truth will set you free.

Pray to know and stay in the truth of God and in His beauty and light!

Have a powerful day!

Day 304
ASK, SEEK, THEN KNOCK

We all have certain hopes, dreams, wishes and desires for which God tells us to ask, seek, and knock. We must be persistent and diligent in our efforts in asking for what we desire.

Matthew 7:7 Keep on asking and it will be given you; keep on seeking and you will find; keep on knocking (reverently) and (the door) will be opened to you.

When children desire, they persistently, and sometimes annoyingly, ask their parents. They employ every effort and every chance until they get what they want. We must also have the tenacity and motivation to continuously ask, seek, and knock with our right wishes to God. When they are aligned with His will, we must believe that it will come.

Matthew 7:8 For everyone who keeps on asking receives; and he who keeps on seeking finds; and to him who keeps on knocking, (the door) will be opened.

Those with great faith and great persistence, beget great rewards. We must do our part in order for God to do His. With prayer, have patience and know that it will come.

Have a believing day!

Day 305
DON'T GIVE INTO YOUR NEGATIVE FEELINGS

Immense pressure, disappointments, accusations and discouragements do not skip over anyone but God tells us not to give into those negative feelings because they can become worse. We must choose to allow His Spirit, who lives inside of us, to give us renewed hope in a new uplifting direction.

2 Corinthians 4:8-9   We are hedged in (pressed) on every side (troubled and oppressed in every way), but not cramped or crushed; we suffer embarrassments and are perplexed and unable to find a way out, but not driven to despair; We are pursued (persecuted and hard driven), but not deserted (to stand alone); we are stuck down to the ground, but never struck out and destroyed.

Our situations can worsen, but God's Spirit is real and active in leading us to a direction of life and freedom. Let us put our trust and focus on our Almighty God for we are more than conquerors with Christ's power residing within us. Rest in His strong arms today.

Have a victorious day!

Day 306
GOD MAKES ALL THINGS POSSIBLE

Let us think a moment about situations in our lives that may have seemed utterly impossible to conquer, but with God's help orchestrating to the minute detail and timing, He made all things possible! What a magnificent impact you can have on others who watch you go through hardships with grace and faith, believing and trusting in God!

Psalm 83:18 That they may know that You, Whose name alone is the Lord, are the Most High over all the earth.

Our job as God's children is to make known His great and almighty name, above all names!

Luke 1:37 For nothing is impossible with God.

Seal that statement in your heart; God's power is unthinkable and unimaginable! Who can fathom our creator? When we allow God to work in our lives, amazing things happen, and we know God gets all the credit. Let us continue to build our trust and faith in Him day by day.

Have a magnificent day!

WHAT IS TRUE FREEDOM

Do you realize that as believers, we have a true freedom within us? The Lord is the Spirit who resides within us, in everything that we think or do. Everything about the Lord is freedom! God made us to be free, with no strings attached!

2 Corinthians 3:17   Now the Lord is the Spirit, and where the Spirit of the Lord is, there is liberty (emancipation from bondage, freedom).

God is all about light and truth! God is not a liar and there is no darkness in Him.

John 8:32   And you will know the truth, and the truth will set you free.   John 8:36   So if the Son liberates you (makes you free men), then you are really and unquestionably free.

Once you know God, you see the truth and are freed! There is no reason to be held captive to sin, bondage or any kind of despair. It would be an insult to God since He sent His Son Jesus to die on the cross for our past, present and future sins. Let us rest assured in thankfulness and gratitude that God set us free in Christ! Praise be to God, our Father!

Have a liberating day!

Day 308
KNOWN BY OUR FRUITS

How are you known to others? In God's word, it says that we are known by our fruits.

Matthew 12:33-34 Make a tree good and its fruit will be good, or make a tree bad and its fruit will be bad, for a tree is recognized by its fruit. You brood of vipers, how can you who are evil say anything good? For out of the overflow of the heart the mouth speaks.

It is obvious the kind of trees we are by the fruits we bear, by the language we use. It is clearly heard by people near us. It is difficult to hide thoughts when the mouth speaks. Let us work on our heart and fill it with good, positive and nurturing thoughts, filled with God's word and His truth in His Spirit. Then in time, the good fruits will be produced and evident to all.

Have a Spirit-filled day!

Day 309
WHO CAN FIGURE OUT OUR OWN HEART?

Do you feel at times that you can't figure out your own heart? The nature of our heart can one day desire everything good, then turn around and desire everything bad!

Jeremiah 17:8 The heart is deceitful above all things, and it is exceedingly perverse and corrupt and severely, mortally sick! Who can know it (perceive, understand, be acquainted with his own heart and mind)? I the Lord search the mind and heart, even to give to every man according to his ways, according to the fruit of his doings.

Only God knows our hearts by searching our intentions. If you're not where you would like to be with your heart attitude, ask God to heal you!

1 John 1:9 If we confess our sins, He is faithful and just and will forgive our sins and purify us from all unrighteousness.

Allow God to do the work in purifying you by confessing your sins to Him! His love and faithfulness to you is unimaginable!

Have a cleansing day!

Day 310
A CLEAR CONSCIENCE FOR A PURE HEART

The importance to have a clear conscience and a pure heart is vital and of great magnitude in God's eyes.

Psalm 19:14 Let the words of my mouth and the meditation of my heart be acceptable in Your sight, O Lord, my Rock and my Redeemer.

A right heart and mind brings us closer to a right relationship with God! It frees us to know Him better and see Him work in our lives. Not having a clear conscience and an impure heart can get in the way of seeing who God is. Let us ask God to clear our consciences by making known to us what needs to be worked on, and believe with His Spirit it will be accomplished!

Psalm 119:9-11 How can a young man keep his way pure? By living according to your word. I seek you with all my heart; do not let me stray from your commands. I have hidden your word in my heart that I might not sin against you.

Our goal is to have a right heart before God so that we may continue to be in line with His will, and to reach our full potential being on our right path in love and in freedom!

Have a clean day!

Day 311
GOD'S SUPERNATURAL STRENGTH OF FLYING

Why do we allow ourselves to get completely exhausted, and then try to gain strength through outside sources? God wants us to go to him for renewed strength and energy, mentally, physically and spiritually!

Isaiah 40:31 But those who wait for the Lord (who expect, look for, and hope in Him) shall change and renew their strength and power; they shall lift their wings and mount up (close to God) as eagles (mount up to the sun); they shall run and not be weary, they shall walk and not faint or become tired).

God restores our bodies, minds and emotions in a way nothing else can compare! As we fix our eyes on God and give Him our focus and attention every day, we will feel the sense of flying, having received His supernatural strength! Imagine that! Let us be encouraged to make it a daily habit for the rest of our lives, to put spending time with God as our first priority! By keeping God number one in your life, you will see Him work magnificently in all areas of your life!

Have a strengthening day!

Day 312
GOD IS WORKING IN US

God is always at work and always working in us.

Philippians 2:13 (Not in your own strength) for it is God Who is all the while effectually at work in you (energizing and creating in you the power and desire), both to will and to work for His good pleasure and satisfaction and delight.

God created us to please and glorify Him. He gives us His power and with Him we are able to continue to live out the plan He has for our lives. The amazing strength we receive from God is out of this world and He is always working within us for His kingdom's purpose.

Have a most purposeful day!

Day 313
HOW PERSONALIZED IS THIS?

God definitely makes us feel special, unique, and of great worth in His eyes! He is always with us and knows our very being, inside and out. How would you like to be on someone's mind all the time? God is always thinking of you!

Psalm 139:13-18   For You formed my inward parts; You covered me in my mother's womb. I will praise You, for I am fearfully and wonderfully made; marvelous are Your works, and that my soul knows very well. My frame was not hidden from You, when I was made in secret, and skillfully wrought in the lowest parts of the earth. Your eyes saw my substance, being yet unformed. And in Your book they all were written, the days fashioned for me, when as yet there were none of them. How precious also are Your thoughts to me, O God! How great is the sum of them! If I should count them, they would be more in number than the sand; when I awake, I am still with you.

Wow! It can't get any more personalized than this! God made you perfect, just the way He created and designed you to be. His unconditional love for us is everlasting.

Have a perfect day!

Day 314
NO IT'S THE OTHER WAY

Don't try to reach perfection by depending upon the flesh. Remember when we first believed in God, it was through faith and leaning on the Holy Spirit.

Galatians 3:3 Are you so foolish and so senseless and so silly? Having begun (your new life spiritually) with the (Holy) Spirit, are you now reaching perfection (by dependence) on the flesh?

Do not put your faith in what you can do, otherwise you will get discouraged and eventually wear yourself out. When at times you fail to do what is right, you can be hard on yourself and it can hinder your walk with God.

We think we are better Christians by how much human effort and work that we put in, maybe thinking that we score more points in people's eyes as well as with God. No, it is by complete dependence in the Spirit of being led, dwelling on God and having the Spirit work within us that brings us to ultimate perfection.

Have a spirit-filled day!

Day 315
DEVELOP GOOD BONES BY HEARING GOOD NEWS

There is one sure way to develop good bones besides taking in calcium! It is by hearing good news!

Proverbs 15:30 The light in the eyes (of him whose heart is joyful) rejoices the heart of others, and good news nourishes the bones.

The bible says that hearing and surrounding yourself with good words, good news, and a good atmosphere has a great impact on developing and nourishing your bones! If you feel that your body is feeling tired or exhausted, then make a conscience effort to surround yourself mentally, physically and spiritually in a positive manner!

Psalm 51:8 Make me to hear joy and gladness and be satisfied; let the bones which You have broken rejoice.

Let us be encouraged to give good news to others as well as taking in good news ourselves! We need to strengthen our bones every day, to have joy and gladness in all circumstances. Life is too short to be wasted!

Have a happy day!

A PERFECT HEART TOWARDS GOD

God is the only one who can see our hearts! People can judge us by our actions, words and performance, but they cannot truly see our *hearts*.

1 Samuel 16:7 But the Lord said to Samuel, Look not on his appearance or at the height of his statue, for I have rejected him. For the Lord sees not as man sees, for man looks on the outward appearance, but the Lord looks on the heart.

It is so important to have a perfect heart towards God. Keep a heartfelt desire to please God, truly loving Him alone!

2 Chronicles 16:9 For the eyes of the Lord run to and fro throughout the whole earth to show Himself strong in behalf of those whose hearts are blameless toward Him.

It does not mean our actions have to be perfect, for God knows that we are imperfect beings, but our hearts are another story.

Proverbs 4:23 Keep and guard your heart with all vigilance and above all that you guard, for out of it flow the springs of life.

Let us examine our heart attitude and make our thoughts pure and right before God. He searches all throughout the earth for people with pure hearts and makes Himself known before them. Let us be encouraged to pray for cleansing, and a good, right heart for a blessed life.

Have a heartfelt day!

Day 317
BE PATIENT WITH GOD'S WILL

Are you ever tempted to take matters into your own hands? It is better for you to wait upon God in wisdom and instruction. Here's an example of being patient with God's will; the story of King Saul wanting to kill the shepherd boy David, out of uncontrollable envy and jealousy towards him being a threat to his kingdom.

2 Samuel 24:3-7 He came to the sheep pens along the way; a cave was there, and Saul went in to relieve himself. David and his men were far back in the cave. The men said, "This is the day the Lord spoke of when He said to you, 'I will give your enemy into your hands for you to deal with as you wish.'" Then David crept up unnoticed and cut off a corner of Saul's robe. Afterward, David was conscience-stricken for having cut off a corner of his robe. He said to his men, "The Lord forbid that I should do such a thing to my master, the Lord's anointed, or lift my hands against him; for he is the anointed of the Lord." With these words David rebuked his men and did not allow them to attack Saul. And Saul left the cave and went his way.

Wow! David had the perfect opportunity to kill Saul right then and there! Instead he chose to do the righteous and noble thing, not wanting to go against his conscience and to wait and obey God. With that in mind, God honored him and made him the next *king*, all in due time! David faithfully trusted in God and in His timing to help him in all matters. Let us remember that God's ways are much better and higher than ours.

Have a yielding day!

Day 318
DOUBTING HINDERS! BELIEVE IN GOD'S GREAT POWER

Why is it that children have an easy time trusting and believing, while doubts can easily confound adults! Maybe situations such as past hurts, disappointments, worries or a lack of faith prevent us from moving forward in our lives. Doubting hinders, and fear can creep in and keep us stuck in the past. We have to know and realize that there is God's great power for those who believe!

Ephesians 1:19 And (so that you can know and understand) what is the immeasurable and unlimited and surpassing greatness of His power in and for us who believe, as demonstrated in the working of His mighty strength.

We cannot limit God in any way. We must believe in the God who created and loved us, and who sacrificed His only son Jesus to save us from our sins. It all starts with believing!

Ephesians 3:20 Now to Him Who, by (in consequence of) the (action of His) power that is at work within us, is able to (carry out His purpose and) do super abundantly, far over, and above all that we (dare) ask or think (infinitely beyond) our highest prayers, desires, thoughts, hopes, or dreams).

God wants us to simply believe in Him!

Luke 8:50 But Jesus, on hearing this, answered him, Do not be seized with alarm or struck with fear; simply believe (in Me as able to do this), and she shall be made well.

Let us put our faith and trust in God by focusing on *who* He is and in His extraordinary power. By believing, we will experience more in our life than we can ever imagine. Praise God!

Have a believing day!

HOW DESPERATE ARE YOU TO GET WELL

Let us have hope when we are in hopeless situations. We must never give up! How desperate are you to get well? Your faith matters!

Mark 5:25-27 And there was a woman who had had a flow of blood for twelve years, And who had endured much suffering under (the hands of) many physician and spent all that she had, and was no better but instead grew worse. She had heard the reports concerning Jesus, and she came up behind Him in the throng and touched His garment. For she kept saying, if I only touch his garments, I shall be restored to health. And immediately her flow of blood was dried up at the source, and (suddenly) she felt in her body that she was healed of her (distressing) ailment.

Wow, what great faith and action! When we see a chance and opportunity to get well, like this lady we must get up on the inside and put all effort, believing that the touch of God's Spirit will heal us, no matter how long you have been in this condition! Let's do our part and leave the rest to God; He promises to take care of us. Have the same faith as this woman in pressing forward towards healing and wholeness. Don't give up no matter what!

Have a hopeful day!

Day 320
HOW CAN WE LOVE OTHERS?

How in the world can we love others? It can seem so hard and challenging at times, especially if they are unlovable! But God commands us to love others in honor of Him!

1 John 4:19-21 We love Him, because He first loved us. If anyone says, I love God, and hates his brother, he is a liar; for he who does not love his brother, whom he has seen, cannot love God, Whom he has not seen. And this command we have from Him; that he who loves God shall love his brother (believer) also.

God gave us a perfect example on how to love others. God woos and lures us into His kindness and greatness! His endless compassion and grace wins us over. Even if others are resistant and can have an ugly nature, keep on loving them as God loved us. When we truly know the depth and love of God's love, out of reverence, respect and awe for Him are we able to *choose* to love others. Let us keep our focus right on God and Who He is; through His Holy Spirit we have the capacity to love. You will be marveled!

Have a loving day!

Day 321
GOD GETS ALL CREDIT

Have you ever been in situations or circumstances where you know that God gets all the credit? You know very well that it was not your ability that made certain things happen!

Psalm 118:23 This is from the Lord and is His doing; it is marvelous in our eyes.

We are truly in awe and in wonder with God's magnificent ways. He loves us dearly and will take care of us always. Let us have a humble and thankful spirit within us, knowing how great our God is. Give Him all praise and glory that He so fully deserves!

Have a glorious day!

Day 322
STEP OUT WITH BOLDNESS

Do you see yourself as overly cautious about certain things, where fear can kick in and can make you paranoid? One thing is for sure, we wouldn't want that feeling to pass along to our children and friends! God is so good, and whatever He provides for us, it is *good*! We may experience growth thru challenges, and when it is aligned with God's will, we must be bold and courageous to do it.

Deuteronomy 1:20-21   And I said to you, You have come to the hill country of the Amorites, which the Lord our God gives us. Behold, The Lord your God has set the land before you; go up and possess it, as the Lord, the God of your fathers, has said to you. Fear not, neither be dismayed.

God tells us not to worry or have any fears. The circumstance of the Amorites appeared frightening, due to the sheer size of the people. God wants us to look beyond the problem and purely trust in Him.

Deuteronomy 1:29-30   Then I said to you. Dread not, neither be afraid of them. The Lord your God Who goes before you, He will fight for you just as He did for you in Egypt before your eyes.

Remember past events and victories with God; He promises to be with you then and now! He already does the fighting for us. All we have to do is step out into the unknown and put our trust in Him. Let us not miss out on our wonderful opportunities given to us by God. Many blessings are to be found there!

Have a conquering day!

SIMPLY SEEK GOOD

Remember the game Hide and Seek? Everyone hides, and one person has to search *everywhere*. God desires for us as His children to seek Him out with all our heart and being!

Hebrews 11:6 But without faith it is impossible to please and be satisfactory to Him. For whoever would come near to God must (necessarily) believe that God exists and that He is the rewarder of those who earnestly and diligently seek Him (out).

God is the source of all good blessings in our life, whether it be material blessings, good health, loving families, peace of mind, restorations, and the list goes on and on. God wants us to draw near to Him, and to go to Him for everything. As we daily seek and acknowledge Him, He continues to guide us in our right path.

Proverbs 3:6 In all your ways know, recognize, and acknowledge Him, and He will direct and make straight and plain your paths.

It is our self-reliance and pride that can get in the way of truly experiencing the abundant rewards and blessings given to us by God.

Proverbs 22:4 The reward of humility and reverent and worshipful fear of the Lord is riches and honor and LIFE.

When we seek and spend time with God in Honor of who He is, the rewards are numerous: A guarantee indeed!

Have a rewarding day!

Day 324
DO NOT WORRY

God tells us not to worry or to be anxious about anything. God has everything under control and His sovereignty rules! The definition of worry is to torment oneself with disturbing thoughts; to feel uneasy and troubled. Worry is a complete waste of time and energy!

Matthew 6:25   Therefore I tell you, stop being perpetually uneasy (anxious and worried) about your life, what you shall eat or what you shall drink; or about your body, what you shall put on. Is not life greater (in quality) than food, and the body (far above and more excellent) than clothing?

There is much value and worth in our being! Don't jump the gun in being worried about tomorrow.

Matthew 6:34   So do not worry or be anxious about tomorrow, for tomorrow will have worries and anxieties of its own. Sufficient for each day is its own trouble.

God gives us peace! Not a worldly peace, but *His* peace.

John 14:27   Peace I leave with you; my (own) peace I now give and bequeath to you. Not as the world gives do I give to you. Do not let your hearts be troubled, neither let them be afraid. (stop allowing yourselves to be agitated and disturbed; and do not permit yourselves to be fearful and intimidated and cowardly and unsettled).

God's peace is available to all!

John 16:33 I have told you these things, so that in Me you may have peace. In this world you will have trouble. But take heart! I have overcome the world.

God assures us with all confidence that He has our back, and has conquered all our trials. Let us rest in His peace today!

Have a serene day!

Day 325
WE HAVE THE POWER TO CHOOSE

Everything about life is made up of choices. Whether the choice is big or small, it greatly affects us and also the generations to come.

Deuteronomy 30:19-20 This day I call heaven and earth as witnesses against you that I have set before you life and death, blessings and curses. Now choose life, so that you and your children may live and that you may love the Lord your God, listen to His voice, and hold fast to Him. For the Lord is your life, and He will give you many years in the land he swore to give to your fathers, Abraham, Isaac and Jacob.

Let us choose to have a well-balanced life. When we are exhausted, we are not good for anybody! Excessive weariness leads us to be in the wrong mindset, which can cause us to make poor choices. That can ultimately make us unhappy and others around us as well. Our feelings are fickle, up one day and down the next; this can also get in the way of making right choices. Let us love and obey God with all our hearts and in everything that we do! Then you will surely live the blessed life and pass it down to others. Great rewards await for those who make the right choices.

Have a decisive day!

Day 326
WATCH OUT FOR THE THIEF

God has already given to us a full abundant life! The enemy's job is to steal it! We must watch out for the thief! He uses all means and any way possible to steal our peace, joy, serenity, goals and dreams, and anything that is good from God. Let us be on guard and not allow Him to steal from us!

John 10:10 The thief comes only in order to steal and kill and destroy. I came that they may have and enjoy life, and have it in abundance (to the full, till it overflows).

We as believers are a big threat to the enemy. He knows all too well the great power that Christ has in our lives. Let us remember who and whose we are, a child of the God most high! Proclaim a conquering spirit and fight the good fight of faith, winning every battle with God's strength residing within us. Victory is already ours! Let us relish our peace and freedom every day of our lives. Don't allow yourself to be tricked and deceived by the scams of the enemy. The power of our thoughts is crucial in the battle to win.

Philippians 4:13 I can do all things through Christ who strengthens me.

Have a beautiful, clear-thinking day!

Day 327
GOD SEES AND NOTICES ALL YOUR EFFORTS

Do you ever feel that whatever good works that you do, no one notices, or that it may not matter? God sees and notices *all* your efforts! They are not in vain. God wants us to be steady and diligent in all our works for Him. In all that we do, we should do it for the glory of God!

Colossians 3:23 Whatever may be your task, work at it heartily (from the soul), as (something done) for the Lord and not for men.

Our motivation should always be to please and glorify God, in honor of Him. It all starts with our attitude!

1 Corinthians 15:58 Therefore, my beloved brethren, be firm, (steadfast), immovable, always abounding in the work of the Lord, knowing and being continually aware that your labor in the Lord is not futile (it is never wasted or to no purpose).

Let us be encouraged not to give up being the best we can be; whether the best parent possible, an excellent worker, doing meaningful house chores, building good relationships etc.. God surely rewards all our efforts and heart attitude. Let us make Him proud.

Have a diligent day!

Day 328
WHATEVER WE FOCUS ON, WE BECOME

Proverbs 23:7 For as he thinks in his heart, so is he.

What we feed off of continues to grow, good things or bad. God tells us to keep His word at the center of our hearts.

Proverbs 4:20-22 ...consent and submit to my sayings. Let them not depart from your sight; keep them in the center of your heart. For they are life to those who find them, healing and health to all their flesh.

We have to feed our hearts with God's word in order to have a good life. The power of our thoughts greatly affects our actions and behavior.

Philippians 4:8 ... whatever is true, whatever is worthy of reverence and is honorable and seemly, whatever is just, whatever is pure, whatever is lovely and lovable, whatever is kind and winsome and gracious, if there is any virtue and excellence, if there is anything worthy of praise, think on and weigh and take account of these things (fix your minds on them).

Let us live a healthy, peaceful, and blessed life by being centered in God's word.

Have a right-focused day!

Day 329
GOD'S PROMISES OF HIS WORD IS
CONTAINED IN OUR HEARTS

No matter how much we may be in denial of who we truly are in God's word, and deny all the promises God holds for us, we cannot contain it in our hearts!

Jeremiah 20:9 If I say, I will not make mention of (the Lord) or speak any more in His name, in my mind and heart it is as if there were a burning fire shut up in my bones. And I am weary of enduring and holding it in; I cannot (contain it any longer).

We must proclaim all of God's promises to us! We must freely accept it and see ourselves as God sees us. He has given us many gifts and talents that we have yet to tap into and use for His glory. When we limit ourselves, we can miss out on all the possibilities and opportunities lying forth in front of us. We must hold true to all of God's promises! Let us be strengthened and be all that God designed us to be. Look into the potential given to you and master it with God's guidance for the use of His glory. As we take the steps of faith into God's word and in His promises, we will be marveled with awe in how God especially created and designed us to be! Proclaim your promise today.

Have an anticipating day!

Day 330
WHAT DRIVES US TO WORK HARD?

What drives us to work hard in doing all that we do? Is it perhaps competition with others, being accepted in our culture, or keeping up with the Joneses? If that is the case, the wise King Solomon who had all the wealth and riches in the world, says it is all vanity!

Ecclesiastes 4:4   Then I saw that all painful effort in labor and all skill in work comes from man's rivalry with his neighbor. This is also vanity, a vain striving after the wind and a feeding on it.

It is useless if all our efforts are in outdoing each other! We must instead enjoy the life given to us as a gift from God.

Ecclesiastes 2:11   Then I looked on all that my hands had done and the labor I had spent in doing it, and behold, all was vanity and a striving after the wind and a feeding on it, and there was no profit under the sun.

How meaningless our works can be if our motives are wrong. Let us have significant substance in all that we do. Let us truly know our meaning and purpose in our lives, by allowing God's Spirit to lead us in the right direction! That itself is a rewarding and a blessed life.

Have a meaningful day!

Day 331
THE IMPORTANCE OF SUPPORT

Why is it that sometimes we may think we can handle things all by ourselves? Maybe in some cases we can, but asking for help and support from another person can be much more satisfying and rewarding!

Ecclesiastes 4:9-10 Two are better than one, because they have a good (more satisfying) reward for their labor; For if they fall, the one will lift up his fellow. But woe to him who is ALONE to lift him up!

We all need each other in one way or another. We can feel isolated, heavy-burdened, and lonely by having the weight of stress and pressure put upon us. God created us to have healthy relationships and support one another! When we have help in different aspects of our lives, we have the freedom to fall, knowing that those around us are there for us to lean on. They can help lift us up by easing our tasks and heavy loads, encouraging us when needed! How wonderful is that? Let us be encouraged not to feel alone in all that we do, but to seek and ask for help in times of need.

Have a supportive day!

ALLOW HOPE TO COME ALIVE AND RESIDE IN OUR HEARTS TODAY

There may be times in our lives when we just want to give up all hope. This is the case in certain situations such as people around us, relationships, within ourselves, etc.. When we have trying times in our lives, we may just want to easily give up! Why? We've come to a place when excessive weariness takes place and we can feel that we no longer have the desire to fight for what is good and right. Hope is all powerful and it promises to never disappoint us!

Romans 5:5 And hope does not disappoint us, because God has poured out His love into our hearts by the Holy Spirit, whom He has given us.

See here? God gives us His everlasting love into our hearts by the Spirit! Let us allow the Spirit to go to work for you. We must believe the power of Christ's resurrection in our lives!

1 Peter 1:21 Through Him you believe in God, who raised Him from the dead and glorified Him, and so your faith and hope are in God.

When we are down and out, let us put our faith, hope and trust in God's word.

Psalm 119:114 You are my refuge and my shield; I have put my hope in your word.

Let us not go by how we feel, rather put our trust in the word of God and do what's right! When we start to change our attitude, the Spirit takes over and the hope that does not disappoint will come alive in your hearts today! Keep on believing, hoping and trusting in all of God's goodness. Allow hope to come alive and reside in our hearts today!

Have a believing day!

GREATEST FIRST COMMAND TO LIVE A GUARANTEED BLESSED LIFE

What does it mean to truly and deeply love someone with all our heart, soul and being? Can it mean that the person is constantly on our minds, which naturally gives us the desire to put all our efforts into loving and pleasing that person with all our strength? God tells us of the great importance of His commandment to simply love Him for who He is!

Deuteronomy 6:4-9 Hear O Israel: The Lord our God, the Lord is one. Love the Lord your God with all your heart and with all your soul and with all your strength. These commandments that I give you today are to be upon your hearts. Impress them on your children. Talk about them when you sit at home and when you walk along the road, when you lie down and when you get up. Tie them as symbols on your hands and bind them on your foreheads. Write them on the door frames of your house and on your gates.

God wants us to constantly be reminded of Him and His great love for us! We should use every opportunity to show our children this great command. God wants reminders everywhere so that we won't forget. Living our lives with the priority of loving God first brings forth the life we all desire to have. A guaranteed blessed life in God!

Have a right thinking day!

Day 334
THE TREASURE OF TRUE HAPPINESS BY A GRATEFUL HEART

Why are some people miserable and nothing ever seems to go their way? Can it be the heart attitude of constant complaints?

Philippians 2:14 Do all things without grumbling and faultfinding and complaining (against God) and questioning and doubting (among yourselves).

Complaining gets us nowhere! It's just wasted energy! Instead, we should redirect our energy and give thanks to God!

Psalm 107:1 O Give Thanks to the Lord, for He is good; for His mercy and loving kindness endure forever!

The treasure of having true happiness is by having a grateful heart! Our roots have to be connected to God for good nourishment.

Colossians 2:6-7 As you have therefore received Christ, (even) Jesus the Lord, (so) walk (regulate your lives and conduct yourselves) in union and conformity to Him. Have the roots (of your being) firmly and deeply planted (in Him, fixed and founded in Him), being continually built up in Him, becoming increasingly more confirmed and established in the faith, just as you were taught, and abounding and over flowing in it with thanksgiving.

As we stay connected and grow in our relationship with God, we develop more of a thankful and grateful heart.

When we find something to complain about, let us immediately readjust and train our attitude towards God's goodness and mercies to us. Think of all the good things in your life!

1 Thessalonians 5:18 Give thanks in all circumstances, for this is God's will for you in Christ Jesus.

That will keep you at peace and at rest and residing in a joy of true happiness!

Have a most grateful day!

Day 335
PROCLAIM YOU RIGHTEOUSNESS IN GOD

Some of us may be a little hard on ourselves thinking, that we are not perfect or right before God. Think again! Only in and through Christ are we righteous! Don't go by Your mistakes and wrong actions on what you do to be right before God, but instead go by who you are! Proclaim your righteousness in God!

2 Corinthians 5:21 God made Him who had no sin to be sin for us, so that in Him we might become the righteousness of God.

See, Christ did all the work for us by overcoming sin for us! God wants to have a love connection with us, through our being righteous in and through Christ! For our sake, God's goodness was shown and sacrificed so that we may be in a right relationship with Him. It is not what we do that makes us righteous, but who we are! Christ did it all for us! Remember who and whose you are, a righteous child of God who loves you so. Let that fact motivate you to live the good life before God!

Have a proclaiming day!

Day 336
GOD'S UNFAILING LOVE AND FAITHFULNESS

Can you imagine having a loved one let you down and hurt you repeatedly, over and over again? How much longer can we endure the disappointments? The question of the depth of our love for the person can arise. God is the only one who has the capacity to have the unfailing love and faithfulness for us! He promises to never let us down or disappoint us in any way!

Psalm 117:1-2 Praise the Lord, all you nations. Praise Him, all you people of the earth. For He loves us with unfailing love; the Lord's faithfulness endures forever. Praise the Lord!

God knows that we can let others down, much less let Him down as well. Still, He created us and knows that we are all broken people, that is why He wants us to lean, depend and rely on His great love for us! The depth of God's love never ceases and His faithfulness to us is everlasting! That is why, because of His never-ending love and kindness towards us, we are drawn and wooed by Him to love and to follow Him! Let us give thanks and praise to God that He loves us no matter what and will continue to the rest of our lives. He promises to be faithful to us!

Have a loving day!

Day 337
DESIRE A SUCCESSFUL LIFE?

Who doesn't want to live a good successful life in pleasantness and in joy? Isn't that what drives us toward success and prosperity? When we strive and pursue to reach for the goals of success and happiness, there comes a time when we may realize that God's ways and His good laws were intended for our ultimate good!

Job 36:11 If they obey and serve Him, they will spend the rest of their days in prosperity and their years in contentment.

Wow, how clear is that? All we have to do is love, obey and serve God, in order to live the good life that God offers to us, in abundance of joy and happiness! What we think may bring us success, can only lead to downfall if it is not aligned with God's will in our lives. We know that we are on the right path when we simply obey God, in loving Him with our whole hearts, mind and strength, and to love and be good to others, doing good. Jesus died for us all so that we may be in a right relationship with God! His sacrifice gives us a channel to live the good right life in Him.

What a blessing that can be if we choose to follow Him! Let us not go by the version of what the world says success is, rather let us have success in God's eyes. It all starts there!

Have a discerning day!

Day 338
SURPRISED BY THIS STRANGE ENDEAVOR

Have you had those times when everything was "peachy keen" and good in your life, then all of the sudden a trial comes your way?

1 Peter 4:12 Dear friends, do not be surprised at the fiery ordeal that has come on you to test you, as though something strange were happening to you.

A big part of growing in Christ is through struggles and trials. We don't like them one bit, but it is there to test the quality of our faith and to build our character, making us stronger in Christ! Allow God to work through you and trust in Him for everything! Always be continually guided by the Holy Spirit and deliverance will come, along with your closeness to God.

Henry Beecher said, "Happiness is not the end of life; character is". It is very important to have a good character, and God knows just what to do to help us build on it! Let's stay in faith and remember: this too shall pass!

Have an enduring day!

Day 339
IS IT TIME FOR YOU TO STEP UP IN FAITH?

Fear seems to always hold us back. We must learn not to be dependent on others to always help us, but to arise in our own faith in God and do what He has called us to do. Is it time for you to step up in faith?

Deuteronomy 31:6   Be strong, courageous, and firm; fear not nor be in terror before them, for it is the Lord your God Who goes with you; He will not fail you or forsake you.

We are never alone. God is always with us, and with His power and strength, we can do anything and everything while we are afraid. We must attempt to conquer our fears with boldness and courage and not allow ourselves to shrink back from anything that is intimidating, frightening or ugly. Let us muster up all our faith in God and be bold to do whatever needs to be done. We are more than conquerors with Christ on our side.

Have a courageous day!

Day 340
GROW IN GRACE

Let us think about some hindrances that may prevent you from growing in God's grace, into the knowledge of God and how to live a Christian life.

2 Peter 3:18 But grow in grace (undeserved favor, spiritual strength) and recognition and knowledge and understanding of our Lord and Savior Jesus Christ. To Him (be) glory (honor, majesty, and splendor) both now and to the day of eternity.

Let us choose to remove whatever may be the "ax" in your life that prevents and hinders you from growing, so that we may continue to grow in grace and flourish into a tree of life. Let us believe that with God's grace, we will be helped in difficult situations that seem impossible to get out of. Victory is ours though His grace and by faith. Grace is available in every situation! Let us praise God and thank Him for living in His grace.

Have a graceful day!

Day 341
DO YOU TRULY WANT TO GET WELL?

Some of us, when sick, seem to become so familiar with being ill that we begin to internalize the ailment to the extent that we believe we will never heal. Some will even adopt a victim mentality. However, do you truly want to get well? It can be a frightening step with fear holding you back and being satisfied in our own misery, but Jesus wants for all of us to take the bold and courageous steps of faith to get well and be free from our bondage.

John 5:5-6   When Jesus noticed him lying there (helpless), knowing that he had already been a long time in that condition, He said to him, do you want to become well? (Are you really in earnest about getting well?

The ailing man responded with nothing but excuses.

John 5:8   Jesus said to him, Get up! Pick up your bed and walk!

That is a direct order coming from Jesus Himself. He knows all the plans and purposes He has for you and wants you to hold on to His promises. If we truly desire to get out of our misery, we must be strong, bold and courageous knowing that God is always with us to give us His strength in our time of weakness. Every moment we spend dwelling in our sickness, whether it be mental or physical, we are wasting our precious life of joy and freedom. Allow God's Spirit to help you muster up all your faith in Him and fuel the fire within you to believing you will heal.

Have a most courageous day!

Day 342
BEING WHO WE ARE BY GOD'S GRACE

If it wasn't for God's wonderful grace, we wouldn't be who we are and where we are today! It was His favor and His blessings to us that made us who we are.

1 Corinthians 15:10 But by the grace (the unmerited favor and blessing) of God I am what I am, and His grace toward me was not (found to be) for nothing (fruitless and without effect). In fact, I worked harder than all of them (the apostles), thought it was not really I, but the grace (the unmerited favor and blessing) of God which was with me.

Receiving and activating God's grace in our lives leaves us with astonishment! We know at times that we are unable to carry on or to do things beyond our control; mentally, physically, and spiritually. But God's grace is always with us to effectively help us along. Boy, do we need it! God knows us so well, that He offers His unmerited favor upon us to be useful for His kingdom's purpose.

Let's stay in faith, knowing God's grace is always with us and sufficient enough to help us become all that we can be. Living in God's grace is the ultimate! Praise God!

Have a reassuring day!

Day 343
HOLD ON TO HOPE

What would this world be without any hope? Hope brings us good things such as excitement, possibilities, recoveries, amazement and joy! Once we get a glimpse of hope in any area of our lives, God's presence from within is stirring us up!..

Hebrews 10:23 So let us seize and hold fast and retain without wavering the hope we cherish and confess and our acknowledgement of it, for He Who promised is reliable (sure) and faithful to His word.

God does not let us down in any way. He knows what is good for us! It is our choice to live in hope or to have despair. We must keep on believing and trusting in Him, even if things do not make any sense. Patience is the key to all good things hoped for! He has a good plan for us and will take care of us! Let us hold tightly without wavering to the hope we affirm, for God can be trusted and He keeps His promises! That's a guarantee!

Have a very hopeful day!

Day 344
CALLOUSED HEARTS?

Have you experienced a callous forming on your hands? It may be from activities such as writing repeatedly with a pencil, playing guitar, or lifting weights, etc.. When the callous develops and grows, it becomes numb! The feeling sensation of the nerves surrounding it is gone! God wants us to be aware and not allow our *hearts* to become calloused.

Matthew 13:15-16 For this people's heart has become calloused; they hardly hear with their ears, and they have closed their eyes. Otherwise they might see with their eyes, hear with their ears, understand with their hearts and turn, and I would heal them. But blessed are your eyes because they see, and your ears because they hear.

Developing a "calloused heart" desensitizes our spirit from truly hearing and seeing God through His word! Even though we may read or listen to His word, we may not truly understand what He is saying to us. It is important to keep our hearts *soft* towards God, to heal our brokenness with His word. Let us not be distracted with the world's influence and business, but keep our hearts and spirits open to receiving God's word. That is where healing is to be found!

Have a blessed day!

Day 345
EMBRACE EACH SEASON

We should see everything as a gift from God; a gift to teach us, smile upon us, discipline us through His love, enjoy with us and to be fruitful. In our lives we go through many different seasons. As the seasons do change eventually, we should have the attitude to embrace each season.

Ecclesiastes 3:1-8 There is a time for everything, and a season for every activity under heaven: a time to be born and a time to die, a time to plant and a time to uproot, a time to kill and a time to heal, a time to tear down and a time to build, a time to weep and a time to laugh, a time to mourn and a time to dance, a time to scatter stones and a time to gather them, a time to embrace and a time to refrain, a time to search and a time to give up, a time to keep and a time to throw away, a time to tear and a time to mend, a time to be silent and a time to speak, a time to love and a time to hate, a time for war and a time for peace.

There is a reason and purpose for every season that we go through in life. Know that God's presence is with you at all times.

Psalm 28:7 The Lord is my strength and my shield; my heart trust in Him, and I am helped. My heart leaps for joy and I will give thanks to Him in song.

Let us all enjoy a personal walk with God as we continue the journey of our blessed lives.

Have an embracing day!

Day 346
TIME TO PRAISE THE LORD

It can be difficult to give someone praise when they surely do not deserve it. But our Almighty God by all means deserves *all* our praise, and more!

Psalm 147:1 Praise the Lord. How good it is to sing praises to our God, how pleasant and fitting to praise him!

Giving praise to God can change us and our circumstances. The practice of praise is fitting and beneficial, and God deserves our praise. Let us sing and meditate on Him day and night! It lifts us up and reminds us on how good and magnificent God is. It puts our focus on God rather than on ourselves and we are reminded to be grateful. A big part of building your relationship with God is fellowshipping with Him by giving Him praise! God surely delights in all our praise.

Have a beautiful day!

Day 347
WHEN WE ARE CURSED, WE BLESS?

Why does God make it so hard to go against our natural fleshly instincts? When we get yelled at or persecuted by people, cut off in traffic, etc., we automatically want to be on their same level at that moment and retaliate with anger!

1 Corinthians 4:12   ...When we are cursed, we bless; when we are persecuted, we endure it; when we are slandered, we answer kindly...

God knows that there will be no peace for us as well as those others in our lives if we do not choose to go against our natural tendencies. We can choose to be an example to others thru the Grace of God.

James 3:2 We all stumble in many ways.

We are not perfect, and people will disappoint us in many ways. People can let us down just like how we may disappoint them without knowing it ourselves! We as believers have Christ's power living inside of us. We have the upper hand to rise above circumstance and respond with God's strength, to act in a way that is pleasing to God! Let us bless people and show mercy, love, and grace to others! Pray for continual wisdom and guidance in this area, for it can be a great challenge to all of us.

Have a kind day!

Day 348
YOU ARE VERY SPECIAL IN GOD'S EYES

Have you ever felt that you were special to another person? Well, you are very special in God's eyes. God's love for you is unimaginable!

Zephaniah 3:17 The Lord your God is in the midst of you, a Mighty One, a Savior (Who saves)! He will rejoice over you with joy; He will rest (in silent satisfaction) and in His love He will be silent and make no mention (of past sins, or even recall them); He will exult over you with singing.

My goodness! What an awesome God we have. God delights in us in every way, for He created us with His great love!

Psalm 139 :16-18 Your eyes saw my unformed substance, and in Your book all the days (of my life) were written before ever they took shape, when as yet there was none of them. How precious and weighty also are Your thoughts to me, O God! How vast is the sum of them! If I could count them, they would be more in number than the sand. When I awoke, I would still be with you.

God's presence is with us from the beginning when we were born, until the very end. He thinks of us all the time! He desires for us to have a love relationship with Him all our lives. He knows us so well and is patient with us, always showing His love and kindness first, so in return we may grow to know and love Him more! Let us soak in His great love today.

Have an endearing day!

Day 349
COME TO YOUR SENSES

All we have to do is to look around us to know that we are living in the last days that Paul had written about. We became self-centered ungrateful, swimming in a culture that describes what Paul warned of! As believers, we must stand firm in God's truth and live by it in gratitude.

2 Timothy 3:1-5 ...There will be terrible times in the last days. People will be lovers of themselves, lovers of money, boastful, proud, abusive, disobedient to their parents, ungrateful, unholy, without love, unforgiving, slanderous, without self-control, brutal, not lovers of the good, treacherous, rash, conceited, lovers of pleasures rather than lovers of God-having a form of godliness but denying its power. Have nothing to do with them.

These are the kind of people we warn our children to stay away from! They can ensnare and trap you into their ways, and without a firm relationship with God we can easily get caught up and go their way! Only God is the everlasting Rock Who satisfies and fulfills us to the fullest in every need!

2 Timothy 3:16-17 All scripture is God-breathed and is useful for teaching, rebuking, correcting and training in righteousness, so that the man of God may be thoroughly equipped for every good work.

It is a fight that is worth the fight until God says, "Well done my good and faithful servant." Let us be that light that shines brightly so that people will see and know God in and through us!

Have a glorious day!

Day 350
DON'T MISS OUT ON YOUR BLESSINGS

There are so many blessings out there for us, but did you know that we can miss out on them by choosing to follow our feelings rather than listening and obeying God's word! Peter gave us a perfect example on how tired and exhausted he was from fishing all day without catching any fish, and so he gave up by the end of the day.

Luke 5:4-7 When He had stopped speaking, He said to Simon (Peter), Put out into the deep (water), and lower your nets for a haul. And Simon (Peter) answered, Master, we toiled all night (exhaustingly) and caught nothing in our nets. And when they had done this, they caught a great number of fish; and as their nets were (at the point of) breaking.

See what they would have missed out on if they chose not to listen and obey to what Jesus commanded! The last thing you want to do when you have worked hard all day and you are completely spent is to go back to work! Going against our feelings in any area of our lives and doing what God wants from us leads us toward a great haul of blessings!

Luke 5:9 For he was gripped with bewildering amazement and all who were with him, at the haul of fish which they had made.

God is asking us to trust Him with all our endeavors, and He will take care of the rest with overflowing blessings! Let us get ready for a great haul and be bewildered by our obedience.

Have an amazing day!

Day 351
SEE WHAT YOU ARE REALLY MADE OF

The only way to truly see what we are made of is by going through tests, challenges and "fires" in our lives! Nobody in their right mind *wants* to experience any kind of discomfort, but that is the way God challenges us. This makes us grow and become useful for His kingdom!

Job 23:10 But He knows the way that I take (He has concern for it, appreciates, and pays attention to it). When he has tried me, I shall come forth as refined gold (pure and luminous).

How can we be made of an extraordinary refined gold if we do not go through hot fires in our lives? God only knows how much we can take and He knows our limitations. If you feel that there is a great challenge ahead of you, know and trust that God will be there to help guide you through in His Spirit! When we are at a point of confusion and things don't make any sense, we must learn to trust in God no matter what. See what happens as a result from our obedience and trust!

James 1:12 Blessed (happy, to be envied) is the man who is patient under trial and stands up under temptation, for when he has stood the test and been approved, he will receive (the victor's) crown of life which God has promised to those who love Him.

Our love for God has to be greater than our skepticism. Let us reach for our crown with great joy and make known God's name above all names! Praise God!

Have an enduring day!

Day 352
WHO ME, PERFECT?

Boy it sounds so farfetc.hed when God tells us we can be perfect. But as believers and with the help of the Holy Spirit within our hearts, little by little every day, we can reach a place of growing into perfection!

Matthew 5:48 You, therefore, must be perfect (growing onto complete maturity of godliness in mind and character, having reached the proper height of virtue and integrity), as your heavenly Father is perfect.

You will be amazed on how much you have grown after you yield to God's Spirit to guide your thoughts and actions!

There is a song called *Jesus is Changing Me!* It says, "Little by little bit every day, little by little in every way, my Jesus is changing me, Oh yes He's changing me! Since I've made that turn about face, I've been walking in His grace, Jesus is changing me!" As we put our focus upon Jesus and seek Him with our whole heart, He is the one who is changing you by His Spirit! Let us not give in to our selfish and stubborn nature, but instead yield to grow into perfection and holiness.

1 Peter 1:15-16 But as the One Who called you is holy, you yourselves also be holy in all your conduct and manner of living.

As we submit and surrender to God, perfection is on its way. Praise God!

Have a bewildered day!

Day 353
NO, IT'S MY PLAN

Have you made certain plans in mind but then got redirected in another direction? What just happened? We must trust in God's ultimate plan for our lives in every way!

Proverbs 19:21 Many plans are in a man's mind, but it is the Lord's purpose for him that will stand.

Children may want to get things their own way by planning out certain ideas and endeavors. That is wonderful, but it is by our great love for them as their parents that we guide and direction them in God's word. Then God's purpose can be done! Our love relationship with God must grow as we continue to trust in Him with our plans; knowing that it is God's will, it *will* happen. If not, then God has a better plan for us!

Job 23:13-14 But He is unchangeable, and who can turn Him? And what He wants to do, that He does. For He performs (that which He has) planned for me, and of many such matters He is mindful.

God cares for us and He wants nothing but good for us. We must trust in our unchangeable, stable, and sovereign God! He loves to see your plans, but He does have a great purpose for you in your life. Let us be encouraged to trust in God's blueprint for our lives and give him the driver's seat in our car. He knows the beginning and the end for our lives so let's enjoy the ride!

Have a purposeful day!

Day 354
PRACTICE AND MODEL YOUR LIFE

Ever wonder why we don't have any peace in certain matters? We hear and read about God's word and truth, but we may not actually *apply* them in our lives!

Philippians 4:9 Practice what you have learned and received and heard and seen in me, and model your way of living on it, and the God of peace (of untroubled, undisturbed well-being will be with you.

If we give it a try and live out what we learn from God's word, then His peace will engulf you and worries and anxieties will cease! Let us practice to keep our minds on things that are good and true, let us learn to be content, let us be empowered by God's strength, for all things are in Christ Who empowers us, and so much more! Let us be encouraged to put into practice, take action, and model our good lives before others in the name of Christ by showing God's character and His heart in and through us.

Have a diligent day in peace!

Day 355
WALK IN THEIR SHOES

It can be difficult to deal with others when we don't know where they are coming from. If we take the time to know the person and their heart, that will determine how we should deal with them!

1 Thessalonians 5:14-15 And I earnestly beseech you, brethren, admonish those who are out of line (the loafers, the disorderly, and the unruly); encourage the timid and fainthearted, help and give your support to the weak souls, (and) be very patient with everybody (always keeping your temper). See that none of you repays another with evil for evil, but always aim to show kindness and seek to do good to one another and to everybody.

We have great advantage with God's Spirit within us to be sensitive and to have compassion for others. Only if we were in their shoes would we understand why they behave the way they do! Let God's love shine through!

Have a compassionate day!

Day 356
OUR RESPONSIBILITY

Can you imagine hearing the last words of someone you greatly respected and admired telling you to "Step up and be responsible"? That is what King David said to his son Solomon.

1 Kings 2:1-4 When the time drew near for David to die, he gave a charge to Solomon his son. "I am about to go the way of all the earth," he said. "So be strong, show yourself a man, and observe what the Lord your God requires: Walk in His ways, and keep His decrees and commands, His laws and requirements, as written in the Law of Moses, so that you may prosper in all you do and wherever you go, and that the Lord may keep His promise to me; 'If your descendants watch how they live, and if they walk faithfully before me with all their heart and soul, you will never fail to have a man on the throne of Israel.'"

It is our responsibility to greatly heed and obey the Lord in every manner, loving Him with all our hearts. It all starts there in order to live well and prosper in everything that we do, anywhere we go! Living a good life with our own journey with God should be shared with the next generations to come.

Psalm 71:18-19 Even when I am old and gray, do not forsake me, O God, till I declare your power to the next generation, your might to all who are to come, your righteousness reaches to the skies, O God, You Who have done great things. Who, O God is like you?

Our personal relationship and love journey with God should be evident to all as an example on how to live a good life in our faith with Him! Let the Spirit of God lead and guide you always!

Have a pondering day!

Day 357
BOAST IN THE LORD

How tempting it can be to take all credit and boast in all our own strength, power, wisdom and wealth. God wants us to take recognition in Him and Him alone as our ultimate source, who gives to us through His kindness and goodness!

Jeremiah 9:23-24 This is what the Lord says; "Let not the wise man boast of his wisdom or the strong man boast of his strength or the rich man boast of his riches, but let him who boast about this; that he understands and knows me, that I am the Lord, who exercises kindness, justice and righteousness on earth, for in these I delight," declares the Lord.

Remember who and whose we are; a child of God, to whom He graciously gives us His goodness and kindness! There will be a time when God gives, and a time when He will take away! Let us give Him all praise and glory that He so deserves, being the source of all our deserving praise. Let our confidence be rooted in God, for we are what we are today because of His love, mercy and grace!

Have a grateful day!

Day 358
IS IT TIME FOR A HEART CHECKUP?

We only have one heart and it is our job to protect it, to keep it healthy in order to live a good life. It can be very difficult to figure out our own hearts, and God sometimes tests our hearts to see where we are at in our lives and what we are made of!

Jeremiah 17:9-10 The heart is deceitful above all things and beyond cure. Who can understand it? I the Lord search the heart and examine the mind, to reward a man according to what his deeds deserve.

How is your lifestyle lately? Is it time to examine your heart and make it right with God? Or perhaps you need to continue nourishing it so that you can be more fruitful! Our heart is of great importance.

Proverbs 4:23 Guard your heart above all else, for it determines the course of your life.

If we want to be aligned with God's will for us, we must guard our hearts with all diligence from evil to keep it pure and right in God's eyes. The course of our lives depends on it! As we pray to God, ask Him to help and direct you and to give you His peace everlasting.

Philippians 4:7 And the peace of God, which transcends all understanding, will guard your hearts and your minds in Christ Jesus.

Let us make daily appointments to check our heart attitude, and make it pleasing to God.

Have a flourishing day!

Day 359
OUR FINITE MINDS

Thank goodness that God does not limit Himself to think like us. That would be very worrisome!

Isaiah 55:8-9 For My thoughts are not your thoughts, neither are your ways My ways, says the Lord. For as the heavens are higher than the earth, so are My ways higher than your ways and My thoughts than your thoughts.

There is no possible way to figure out the mind of God to the fullest, and that's OK. By just trusting in the all knowing, infinite, almighty God is good enough for me! He knows the very number of hairs that you have on your head. He knows your past, present, and future! He wants you to believe, rely, and depend on Him for everything! He knows what the best is for you and cannot wait to give it to you! All He asks of you is to know Him, love Him, worship, please and glorify Him. As you open up your mind and heart to Him, you get a wonderful taste of His being. That itself should motivate you to desire to get to know Him more and more each day.

Have a heavenly day!

Day 360
THE IMPORTANCE OF GOOD COMPANIONS

It is very important for us to be aware and take caution of whom we choose to be close companions with. Foolish influences of some people can disrupt our walk with God, and we can be deceived into following their ways of thinking, behaving and acting in foolish and unjust manners.

Proverbs 12:26   A righteous man is cautious in friendship, but the way of the wicked leads them astray.

Let's be cautious and set up boundaries.

Proverbs 14:7-8 Stay away from a foolish man, for you will not find knowledge on his lips. The wisdom of the prudent is to give thought to their ways, but the folly of fools is deception.

God always wants us to think about our ways of living. Living in a good and right manner gives honor and glory to God, along with abundant blessings.

Proverbs 13:20 He who walks with the wise grows wise, but a companion of fools suffers harm.

Let us not be deceived into foolish talk and behaviors, but instead be wise in all our doings.

Proverbs 19:8 He who gets wisdom loves his own soul; he who cherishes understanding prospers.

Let us keep learning and growing in the kingdom of God, and be wise with all our companions!

Have a discerning day!

Day 361
MIND YOUR OWN BUSINESS

Sometimes the more we hear about others through gossip, sharing with one another, or even prayer requests, etc., it can get us *down, defeated* and in *misery*! Watch out and be aware of their entanglements! Let us have compassion for others but do not allow yourselves to get so entangled in their business, which can cause you to lose your peace and joy!

1 Thessalonians 4:11   To make it your ambition and definitely endeavor to live quietly and peacefully, to mind your own affairs, and to work with your hands, as we charged you.

Let us focus on our own life and continually work to build it up in a Godly manner, away from unsettling matters, misery and defeat! The more we hear of other people's lives, good or bad, it can be a distraction from appreciating our *own* lives! Let us choose not to dwell on other people's business, and do not allow it to consume you! Let us use great discernment when we hear about others!

Enjoy your life freely and stay on course for what God has planned for you.

Have a serene day!

People that may *appear* fearless and brave to others are not immune to their own weaknesses and fears.

2 Samuel 17:10 And even he who is brave, whose heart is as the heart of a lion, will utterly melt.

We are not alone with our challenges! God is always with us to help us in times of need. Let us call out to Him to be our strength!

Philippians 4:13 I have strength for all things in Christ Who empowers me (I am ready for anything and equal to anything through Him Who infuses inner strength into me; I am self-sufficient in Christ's sufficiency).

It may be hard to ask for help when we think we are able to handle things on our own, but God wants us to keep our connection with Him and to remember that He is our everything.

The story of Samson and Delilah reminds us that even though Samson had incredible strength and bravery, he knew the source was from God. He used it for God's glory! It was when Delilah tricked him into giving away the secret to his strength (the long locks of his hair God gave him), she then had the opportunity to cut it off. He lost all strength and became weak as any normal man. When Samson came to his senses, He cried out to God in faith for renewed strength to show God's power to the people in and through him. God saw his humble, good heart and restored his strength, helping him in his time of need. God's power and glory was shown through Samson's incredible strength once again!

Let us recognize our strengths and weaknesses, and remember that God is always with us no matter what!

Have a strong day!

Day 363
THE GOODNESS OF OUR AWESOME GOD

Let us take notice on how evident God's goodness is in our lives!

Psalm 34:8-9 Taste and see that the Lord is good; blessed is the man who takes refuge in Him. Fear the Lord, you His saints, for those who fear Him lack nothing.

We are so fulfilled in God's goodness as long as we are in reverential fear and awe in Him and in Him alone!

Psalm 48:1 Great is the Lord, and most worthy of praise, in the city of our God, His holy mountain.

Our God is surely an awesome, sovereign God who deserves all our praise. Let us always remember to place Him in the position He deserves; first and foremost. Magnify His supreme greatness, rather than in our minute problems! God represents all the goodness in our lives that He so graciously gives to us. Let us have a constant heart of thankfulness, gratitude and praise to our marvelous Lord and Savior!

Have a most blessed day!

Day 364
GROWING UP AND FLOURISHING

How old are you on the inside? They say that age is just a number, but God wants us to grow up in Him *spiritually* so that we may be like Him in all aspects of our lives. If we choose to be like children in our ways and manner, we will be tossed back and forth with no real substance and vitality.

Ephesians 4:14-15 Then we will no longer be infants, tossed back and forth by the waves, and blown here and there by every wind of teaching and by the cunning and craftiness of men in their deceitful scheming. Instead, speaking the truth in love, we will in all things grow up into Him Who is the Head, that is, Christ.

God wants us to take up challenges head on so that we may grow up in Him! He will always be with us to give us strength and guidance, never leaving or forsaking us. Have no fear, for fear holds us back! Let us be strong and courageous to step forward in our lives and keep on growing and flourishing in Christ name.

Psalm 92:12 The righteous will flourish like a palm tree, they will grow like a cedar of Lebanon; planted in the house of the Lord, they will flourish in the courts of our God.

If you feel stagnant in your life, pray that God's hand may be upon you to lead you towards a life of His richness and blessings. Just trust and grow in Him, every day! Let us be proactive on feeding and nourishing our souls, for therein lies true beauty!

Have a flourishing day!

Day 365
ENJOY YOUR LIFE TO THE FULLEST

We should always remember that every day is a true gift from God!

Psalm 118:24 This is the day which the Lord has brought about; we will rejoice and be glad in it.

Dr. Bruce Lipton says, "Your perception controls your behavior." We may never know the number of our days but we should live with great intention, great passion and abundant gratefulness to enjoy our days here on earth!

Psalm 90:12 Teach us to number our days aright, that we may gain a heart of wisdom.

Taking wise actions helps us to enjoy our lives. Many people live with much regret; they seem to say to themselves, "I should have or could have done that!" Let's be encouraged not to have that mentality, but treasure and number our days to enjoy our life to the fullest *today*! Jesus said that He came to give us life abundantly till it overflows to the fullest. It's a sad position to be in when we waste the life that God has given to us. God has created us for great meaning and purpose. Let us say the words, "I love you" and "Thank you," and speak life into other people! Let's make a difference all around us, because we matter a great deal and we have the capacity to shine forth God's beauty within us. Let us be encouraged today to go for our hopes, dreams and visions, and have no regrets as long as we can help it! There are no excuses that we can come up with to prevent us to be all that we can be in God's eyes. In and through Christ we are more than conquerors!

Have a gratifying day!